The ABA
Practical Guide
to Drafting Basic

# Islamic

Finance Contracts

Dena H. Elkhatib

ABA Section of
**International Law**
*Your Gateway to International Practice*

Cover design by Jill Tedhams/ABA Publishing.

Page layout by Quadrum Solutions.

The materials contained herein represent the opinions of the authors and editors and should not be construed to be the views or opinions of the law firms or companies with whom such persons are in partnership with, associated with, or employed by, nor of the American Bar Association or the ABA Section of International Law unless adopted pursuant to the bylaws of the Association.

Nothing contained in this book is to be considered as the rendering of legal advice for specific cases, and readers are responsible for obtaining such advice from their own legal counsel. This book and any forms and agreements herein are intended for educational and informational purposes only.

Printed in the United States of America.

16 15 14 13 12     5 4 3 2 1

Library of Congress Cataloging-in-Publication Data

Elkhatib, Dena H.
The ABA practical guide to drafting basic Islamic finance contracts / by Dena H. Elkhatib.
     p. cm.
Includes bibliographical references and index.
ISBN 978-1-61438-619-3 (alk. paper)
1. Contracts (Islamic law) 2. Finance (Islamic law) I. American Bar Association. Section of International Law. II. Title.
KBP940.2.E43 2012
346.07—dc23

2012022529

# Dedication

I dedicate this book to all the amazing people in my life and most specifically my parents, Hasan and Maysoon, my siblings Abeer and Mahmoud Faisal, and my sister-in-law Diala.

# Foreword

The Islamic finance industry is often unfamiliar to many lawyers, bankers, and businesspersons. But its influence and growth are hard to deny, with assets estimated by some to be anywhere from US $882 billion to US $1 trillion and an annual growth rate of approximately 14 or 15 percent.[1] As the author notes, Islamic finance is a long-term industry with great potential: it is "a strong and viable alternative in the marketplace and should not be underestimated."[2] Its activities are thought to affect twenty percent of the world's population.[3]

In a world of financial crises and fiscal uncertainty, many individual and institutional investors are turning to instruments of Islamic finance in hope of finding safe, stable, and secure investments. Some investors see the asset-based financing principles of Islamic finance as a desirable alternative to volatile investments.[4] Indeed, Investment and business opportunities throughout the Middle East may encompass Islamic financing principles. France, the United Kingdom, and other European governments and financial institutions have begun adjusting their banking laws and practices to accommodate shariah-compliant transactions.[5] Other countries around the world may follow their lead as more is learned about those aspects of Islamic finance that can increase stability in financial markets. And individual investors interested in stable financial investments will increasingly notice finance tools that may be labeled as Shariah-compliant.

Dena H. Elkhatib, the author of this book, is a U.S.-trained lawyer now working in the United Arab Emirates. At the time of the publication of this book, she is a Co-Chair of the Islamic Finance Committee of the American Bar Association Section of International Law. She has previously authored articles to introduce basic principles of Islamic finance to audiences unfamiliar with terms such as *fiqh*, *sukuk*, and *murabaha*. In this book, she expands that previous work and provides readers with a useful introduction and reference guide to Islamic finance and Islamic finance contracts.

Part I of this book introduces Islamic finance and some basic principles of Islamic law. This section explains Shariah and its fundamental sources:

---

1. *See, e.g.,* Dena H. Elkhatib and Pierre M. Gaunaurd, *Islamic Finance,* ___ Int'l Law. ___, ___ (2012).

2. Dena H. Elkhatib, Practical Guide When Drafting Islamic Finance Contracts [56] (2012).

3. *Id.* at [5].

4. Elkhatib & Gaunaurd, *supra* note 1, at ___.

5. *Id.* at ___.

the Holy *Qu'ran*, the *Sunnah* of the Prophet, the consensus statements on points of law known as the *Ijama*, and the legal reasoning by analogy known as *Qiyas*. She also explains the historical struggle for understanding by judges and scholars known as *Ijtihad*, reliance on previous interpretations known as *Taqlid*, and considerations of public welfare known as *Maslaha* or *Mursalah*. This introduction also briefly explains the different schools of Islamic thought as well as an important cautionary note: there is no universal regulating body for Islamic finance and that around the world investors may find varying enforcement and practices of Islamic finance.

Part II of this book reviews the basic elements of Islamic contracts as well as the different types of contracts in Shariah law, such as the *wa'd* (unilateral promise), *muwaaa'adeh* (bilateral promise), and *aqd* (contract). Because Shariah law prohibits an individual from entering into two simultaneous contracts regarding the same object, the distinctions may be quite important.[6] This part of the book explains fundamental principles such as fairness, freedom of contract, and avoiding illegal subject matter in contracting. Of particular interest to many readers will be the extended discussion of *Riba*, a complex word that has been the source of much controversy because it is thought to prohibit the payment of interest,[7] and the regulation of *Gharar*, the "uncertainty or speculative practice in a contract."[8] This part also discusses the important contract principles of good faith, honesty, and fair dealing.[9]

Part III examine different types of Islamic finance structures, such as *Murabaha*, the controversial *Tawarruq* transactions, the finance and leasing agreements known as *Ijara*, the profit-loss sharing agreements known as *Musharaka* or *Mutanaqisa*, and the often short-term principal-agent contracts known as *Mudarabah*.

If any of these terms are unfamiliar to you, this book will be a welcome resource. Its explanations and illustrations will assist your understanding of Islamic finance and provide you with a basis for additional research for specific issues that may arise. As the field of Islamic finance continues to expand, so too must our appreciation of the issues it raises in a wide variety of transactions across the globe.

Mark E. Wojcik
Professor of Law
The John Marshall Law School
Chicago, Illinois UA

---

6.    ELKHATIB, *supra* note 2, at [14].
7.    *Id.* at [17-19].
8.    *Id.* at [19-21].
9.    *Id.* at [22-23].

# Contents

# PART III: TYPES OF ISLAMIC FINANCE STRUCTURES

# Contents

# Acknowledgment

There are several people and organizations that I wish to express my sincere appreciation and gratitude for their assistance in making this book come to fruition and for all of their support. The first is Professor Mark Wojcik, who is a driving force and inspiration always, a dear mentor and friend. Thank you for all of your support, encouragement and ultimately you forcing me to expand my horizons. The second is Richard Paszkiet for his ultimate patience and guidance during this process. Rick, you are amazing at what you do and your patience in working with me long distance will never be forgotten. Lastly, I am highly appreciative of the support of the American Bar Association and those responsible on a daily basis to ensure that the completion and success of this publication. Many thanks to you all and to the readers who have decided to take this journey.

# Introduction

Welcome to Islamic finance and the basic knowledge that you will need to write an Islamic finance contract. If you have picked up this book, it is either out of curiosity about what makes an Islamic finance agreement different from a conventional financial agreement or it is a practice that you or members of your firm are contemplating entering into.

There are several things we will discuss in order to help provide a fuller perspective of not only the practice, but also the theory of Islamic finance. Part I is dedicated to understanding what Islamic finance is, what sources are relied on, and what its place is in the current global financial markets. This section will also discuss the future possibilities of Islamic finance.

Part II is dedicated to understanding the important elements in any Islamic contract. These elements are the foundation of an Islamic finance contract and the basics for any contract that requires compliance with Islamic law. Finally, Part III will discuss the various types of Islamic contracts and how they are structured. In that part, we will discuss various elements that are used to distinguish the type of structural arrangement between the parties. Part IV, the conclusion, is necessary in any book.

In the back of the book you will find an Appendix with each type of structure outlined in a chart format to assist with your understanding of the various structures. Hopefully, you will find this book easy to read and useful in your daily practice or in training other lawyers in Islamic finance.

# Part I: What is Islamic Finance?

# What is Islamic Finance?

In order to truly understand the subject, we must start with the most basic question: what is Islamic finance?

Approximately 35 years ago, a financial institution emerged in the global marketplace and began to distinguish itself from conventional financing.[1] This new field, initially referenced as Islamic banking, has assumed the new title of Islamic finance.[2] A new concept was being introduced—the application of Islamic Shariah financing principles to govern transactions. Today, the Islamic finance industry has grown into US$800 billion in assets globally.

In 2005, it was reported that the number of Islamic Finance institutions had risen to over 300 institutions in 75 different countries both in the East and West.[3] In 2008, the United Kingdom was ranked as one of the top 15 countries managing Shariah-compliant products.[4] The growth in this new industry is not finished, as it is remaining steadfast during the global financial crunch. Until the global credit crisis in 2007, it was reported that the estimated annual growth of Islamic finance worldwide was 10 percent to 15 percent annually. The activities of these financial institutions affected over 20 percent of the global population.

The rapid expansion of Islamic finance is diversified from retail banking to capital markets, including mutual funds, insurance (takaful), and Islamic branches of conventional banks. Islamic finance is also becoming the tool utilized by global organizations in expanding foreign direct investments, stimulating underdeveloped economies, and leveraging the stability of the Shariah-compliant financial instrument in the marketplace. Islamic finance is gaining interest as a prominent financial structure and a substitute to the conventional structure in an ever-growing global Muslim population.

Islamic finance is built on several fundamental Shariah principles, the core of which resides in the basic principle of Islamic economics—fairness. Fairness of a contract is an important element that should be the underlying principle in every Islamic transaction. The basic tenets of an Islamic financial structure take into account important principles such as Shariah-compliant contracting rules, business ethics, property laws, and financial restrictive laws (usury). In order to understand what Islamic finance is, it is important to gather a basic understanding of the underlying principles in Shariah law (Islamic law). The next section will discuss Shariah law and what it means. Note that as a quick guide to Islamic finance these are cursory elements to help establish a foundation necessary to understanding the basic structures of Islamic financial transactions.

## What is Shariah Law?

It is important to understand the difference between Islamic theory and legal practice in the Middle East. Islam is a religion similar to that of Christianity and Judaism. There are no borders to the religion and each individual practices the religion by his or her understanding. It must also be understood that similar to Western law, which was derived initially from ethical codes outlined in Scriptures, the same is true in the Middle East.

Each country in the Middle East applies a form of secular and Islamic law (Shariah). Shariah law is defined as the fundamental Islamic rules that Muslims reference when deciding whether something is permissible. Shariah law is defined as Islamic jurisprudence. Each Middle Eastern country functions with its own laws and regulations. Each has a blend of Shariah and a Western influence of either common or civil law jurisdictions. In order to understand practices in the Middle East, you must understand the influences of Shariah law in the local law of the country in which you practice.[5] This understanding is important to ensure not only that the contracts comply with the law of the jurisdiction, but also that they are enforceable within the appropriate jurisdiction.

It is important to understand where the laws and principles of Shariah law originate. These laws are initially derived from the Quran and teachings of the Prophet Muhammad.[6] Islam is taught and viewed by Muslims as a comprehensive way of life, encompassing all relationships and transactions—both personal and business.[7] In the course of Islamic history, a political rift emerged within the Muslim empire and, as a result, Muslims were divided into sects Shia and Sunni. Several other religious factions have grown throughout the years as well. We will focus on the Sunni interpretations.

The majority of Muslims are Sunni. Under the Sunni ideology, there are four methods in which the details of the laws are applied. All four methods are accepted in the Sunni practice. These four methods do not vary on the underlying faith principles; rather, the variation is derived from the specific interpretation and practices. For example, when a Sunni prays. does he place his hands by his side or overlapping across the chest? This difference does not affect the fundamentals of the prayer; rather, it provides alternative methods in the practice of these beliefs. So a Sunni Muslim may pray as prescribed by one method and conduct business in accordance with another and still be considered a Sunni.

Islamic law is believed to provide an inclusive legal, political, and religious system.[8] The overall principles are typically broad, which opens the prospect of multiple interpretations. It is fundamental to understand that Islamic law does not accept any rule that negates a principle.[9] Rather, Shariah law assumes that "all things are originally permitted unless they are legally prohibited."[10] This is the area in which a struggle between secular laws and Shariah laws occurs.[11] In some instances, due to this conflict there are inconsistent rulings on fundamental issues, further complicating business relationships.[12]

Islamic Shariah law is based on various hierarchies of religious sources.[13] You may wonder why it is important to understand sources when drafting a document. Understanding where the law stems from, that is, from which source and the degree of its authority, will help provide a clearer understanding in practice.

The fundamental sources referenced in Islamic law are first the Quran and next the Sunnah of the Prophet Mohammad. These two sources are the fundamental and primary sources used as principles in the way of life for Muslims.[14] These sources are the initial references utilized when researching or discussing any topic.[15] After the death of the Prophet Mohammad, there was a need for continuous interpretation of the Quran and Sunnah.[16] This led to the development of secondary sources of authority used to interpret them. These secondary supplemental sources used to understand and develop Shariah law are Ijma, Qiyas, Ijtihad, Taqlid and Maslaha.

## *The Quran*

The primary source referenced when deciphering Shariah law is the Quran, the Holy Scripture for Muslims.[17] It is also the most authoritative.[18] The Quran is believed to be the divine words of God revealed through His last messenger and Prophet Mohammad.[19] The Quran was revealed to the Prophet Mohammad over a span of 22 years.[20] Only a few verses were revealed at a time.[21] As each verse was revealed, it was written, preserved, and memorized by the various Muslim companions.[22] The total text of the Quran is comprised of 114 Suras (chapters).[23] These chapters were arranged during the lifetime of the Prophet Muhammad in order of length in the Quran. The Quran does not read in any other sequential or particular order.

Upon the death of the Prophet Mohammad, the first Caliph, Abu Bakr, instructed that all written pages of the Quran be collected into one manuscript.[24] This manuscript was entrusted to the widow of the Prophet.[25] Several years later, the third Caliph, Othman ibn Afa'an, made five copies from the original compilation of the Quran.[26] He then sent them to the various corners of the expanding Islamic Empire for preservation and reference.[27] The Quran used today and every Quran printed is an identical copy of the originals.[28] Muslims accept the literal meaning of the Quran, but scholars also analyze the context in which each verse was revealed.

## Sunna of the Prophet

The second source of authority in Shariah is the Sunna.[29] The Sunna is the collection of words, sayings, or actions of the Prophet Mohammad.[30] The word Sunna means an established practice to be followed.[31] The Sunna is a clarification and a confirmation of the rules prescribed within the Quran.[32] It exemplifies an accepted holy tradition as dictated by the Prophet Muhammad.[33] Furthermore, the Sunna establishes rules for for matters which are silent in the Quran.[34]

The Sunna is regarded as a model of application of the rules and laws within Islam.[35] It is an indication of the manner in which someone should conduct himself or herself.[36] These traditions of the Prophet were compiled and related by his companions. The Sunna references details of the Prophet's conduct or words. From this conduct, Shariah extrapolates what practices are acceptable or unacceptable in Islam. The Sunna was compiled with meticulous thoroughness in confirming the source and character of each speaker and confirming the details of each action prior to legitimizing its authority.

## Ijama

Ijama is defined as the consensus on a point of law by those authorized to interpret the Quran and Sunna.[37] It is important to understand that not all persons are viewed as having the authority to interpret the Quran and Sunna. These qualified persons are called Mujtahideen, qualified jurists. They are notable scholars who have both the requisite intellect and integrity to attain such a position within the community.[38] Furthermore, the doctrine of consensus in Sunni Islam requires the unanimous opinion of the Sunnite community through the use of qualified scholars in any generation on a religious matter. This consensus is considered to be an authority and is to be accepted by all Muslims in later times."[39] Any ruling by the Mujtahideen must comply with both the Quran and the Sunna.[40]

## Qiyas

The next secondary source is called Qiyas[41] Qiyas is defined as a strict reasoning by analogy.[42] Qiyas is only used when no rule may be found in the first three sources.[43] Furthermore, Qiyas is also used if there is a conflicting point clearly established from the Quran, Sunna or Ijma.[44] Qiyas does not form a precedent to be followed since its rules are applied to the facts within a narrow context.[45] Therefore, unlike the common law systems of the West, Islam does not have legal binding precedent.[46] Rather, it is more fact-specific and relies on the application of the law directly to those facts. In the event that the law and facts are not clear, than Qiyas is used to analogize the rule in relation to the specific facts.[47] The court may abstain from applying a rule due to the lack of similarities of the situation.[48]

An example of this method is the prohibition of drugs in Islam. There is no clear verse in the Quran or the Sunna of the Prophet that indicates that drugs are forbidden.[49] Rather, contemporary jurists issued an edict prohibiting the use of drugs by using the method of Qiyas. Scholars drew an analogy analyzing the effects of drugs and determined that the effects of drug use are similar to those of alcohol consumption.[50] Alcohol in Islam is forbidden in any quantity. The reasoning for such a prohibition on the consumption of alcohol is due to its ability to alter a person's reasoning; similarly, the use of drugs also alters a person's reasoning. Therefore, the same reasoning (illa) used for the prohibition of alcohol may be transferred and applied to the prohibition of drugs in Islam.[51] As a result, it is agreed that the use of drugs in Islam is prohibited.

## Ijtihad

A third secondary source in Islamic Shariah is Ijtihad.[52] Ijtihad[1] is defined in Arabic as "the struggle for understanding."[53] The method to struggle for understanding is employed by Islamic judges or scholars in an attempt to resolve a situation that was not previously dealt with in any of the above sources.[54] The scholars must weigh the implications of the situation and struggle to understand how best to apply the Shariah laws outlined in the above sources. Again, it is important to note that only those perceived to be worthy to possess integrity and intellect as religious scholars may attempt to interpret the Quran and Hadith.[55] Therefore, this source of authority is limited to those individuals.

Between the tenth and fifteenth century, Islamic scholars "closed the doors of ijtihad."[56] The closing of the doors marked the ending of independent reasoning in Shariah.[57] Since that time, no scholars have practiced Ijtihad. This "freezing" of the law is argued by some to be the reason that Shariah

---

1.  There is a misconception that the derivative of this word (jihad) exclusively means "holy war." The word ijtihad and the derivatives all reference a struggle—people may struggle with their inner self, with society, with their religious beliefs, with their studies, etc. So it is important to be aware that this word refers only to a struggle.

has not developed adequately since that time.[58] The loss of Ijtihad has restricted the growth of Shariah law and the clarification of various legal principles, such as intellectual property protections.[59]

Historians have commented that Shariah law is still "locked in the world view that then existed" in the fifteenth century and has since been unable to evolve with the various social and economic needs of society.[60] Many have further indicated that this is reflected in the lack of economic growth in many countries throughout the Middle East.[61] The use of the legal tool of reasoning Ijtihad was no longer available and as a result Islamic scholars are dependent on the final and last form called Taqlid.

## *Taqlid*

Taqlid is the "submissive acceptance of an earlier interpretation" of the Shariah law.[62] Since the doors of independent reasoning were closed, Islamic scholars are not given the authority to develop and reason based on Ijtihad. Therefore, the Islamic scholars of today must rely on previous interpretations. Taqlid is a method that some criticize as blind following. It is utilized when an individual did not learn or understand the practices of Islam and therefore relies on previous interpretation. This path is debated among various scholars in that there is a belief that there should be no blind following in Islam.

## *Maslaha/Mursalah*

A fourth secondary source in Islamic Shariah is Masalaha or Mursalah. Masalaha/mursalah may be described as "in the interest of the public."[63] This form of analysis is only used after all other sources are exhausted. Masalaha is based on the belief that "the basic purpose of legislation in Islam is to secure the welfare of the people by promoting their benefits or by protecting them against harm."[64] Islamic jurists maintain "five main goals of Shariah": "safeguarding and promoting the individual's faith; life; intellect; posterity; and wealth."[65] Islamic law presumes that the interests of individuals and the community correspond with these goals.[66]

Masalaha requires the following conditions to be met in order to avoid any arbitrary decision.[67] First, there must be a reasonable probability that the benefits of the new rule outweigh any potential harm.[68] Second, the interest must be such that the benefit or the harm prevented protects a significant number of members of society.[69] Last, the new opinion must not contradict or negate expressly or impliedly any values or legal principles established by the Quran and Sunna.[70]

# What are the Different Sects?

*Shi'a and Sunni*

Similar to all global religions, differences over time have created rifts among the Muslims.[71] The result is multiple groups or sects that identify themselves as Muslims. The most notable division is between the Shi'ites and Sunnis.[72] As discussed earlier, we will focus on the Sunni Muslims.

Sunni Muslims follow one of four different religious schools of thought known as Mathahab, meaning rights.[73] Each Mathhab is named after its recognized scholar.[74] The Sunni schools of thought are Hanafi, Shafi', Maliki, and Hanbali. These schools of thought do not differ from the basic principles and fundamentals of the religion; rather, they provide varying guideposts for ways in which the religion may be applied to one's life. We will not delve deeply into the teachings of each specific Mathahab. Instead, we will try to build a fundamental understanding of Islamic finance and its teachings as a whole.

Another important point to understand about Islam and its teachings is that although there are guidelines for finance, trade, and economics, Islam is a faith. As a faith, it is not bound by borders. Rather, it is an influencer in legislative practices in various regions of the world, but it is not the exclusive law of that region or country. Islam is not a country, nor a defined place with branches of government. Islam is a faith of 1 billion people scattered throughout the world. Therefore, there are certain important elements that are lacking in regard to Islamic finance, such as a universal regulating body or authority overseeing all Islamic finance practices within the world and standardizing the practice and enforcement principles. As such, one will find varying enforcement of practices of Islamic finance throughout the world. Overall, however, the underlying principles of Islamic finance are recognized and should not be disregarded in contracting.

There are many global sources and authorities in Islamic finance. The most recognized organization that has developed a guide to Islamic finance principles is the Accounting and Auditing Organization for Islamic Financial Institutions (AAOIFI). However, there is no verification or enforceability mechanism to ensure global compliance or enforcement with AAOIFI standards, since it is not a governing body.[75] Several jurisdictions have, however, adopted AAOIFI standards, which complement the International Financial Reporting Standards.[76]

# Part II: Basic Elements to any Islamic Contract

# What is the Typical Practice of Islamic Finance?

The typical practice in Islamic finance is that the relevant organization ("Bank") (finance company, commercial bank, Islamic bank, etc.) seeks to develop a product line which is Shariah-compliant. The Bank will appoint a Shariah board that may vary from one member to five members. The number of Shariah advisors will depend on the local laws of the jurisdiction or on the discretion of the Bank. The Shariah advisor helps provide the consumer with assurance that the Bank is complying with Shariah principles.

The documents drafted for the Bank transactions will be reviewed with respect to Shariah compliance. The Shariah advisors may request revisions to each of the documents to comply with various Islamic finance principles. It should be noted that just because a Shariah advisory board from another institution accepted the same contract does not ensure a universal acceptance for all Shariah advisors. Each Shariah board of each Bank works independently. Therefore, there is a discretionary aspect to the current practice of Islamic finance and the acceptance of a document as Shariah-compliant. Furthermore, the qualifications of a Shariah advisor do not necessarily require an individual who is legally trained. Therefore, there are instances in which it will be important to discuss varying aspects of the contract with the Shariah advisors, if possible.

An important tip in relation to drafting Islamic finance contracts is learning the art of drafting a contract that considers the enforcement aspects within the applied jurisdiction. The contract should conform to the Shariah regulations and still be enforceable within the governing law jurisdiction. As you will see in this book, Islamic finance contracts are governed by similar contracting principles globally recognized. Therefore, the only concern is to conform parts of the contract when drafting to encompass the jurisdictional elements for complete enforceability of the contract.

# Where did Islamic Finance Originate?

There is evidence of trade and economic regulation from the inception of Islam. Islamic finance law is developed mostly from the secondary Islamic sources discussed in Part I. There is a strong reliance on the learned scholars to pass a fatwa to help clarify areas of uncertainty in the practice of Islamic finance. A fatwa is a religious decree that is issued by a religious scholar. Since Islam has no independent enforcement powers as a religion, the issuance of the fatwa and its application is dependent on people willingly adhering to the clarification and the new rules.

There is no one official body that regulates the Islamic finance industry. Rather, there are various learned scholars who issue a fatwa, sometimes contradictory rules, which results in discrepancies in the exact application of what is construed to be the rules. Also, there is a lack of standardization within the Islamic finance industry. But this lack of standardization does not impair the basic principles that all Islamic finance contracts must adhere to in order to be properly compliant. There is a growing movement and a desire within the Islamic finance industry to find a manner to regulate the industry as a whole. However, this is proving to be a challenge and will take time. Most important, there is a growing fear that unless the industry shapes itself, it will slowly be consumed by the conventional finance practice. Therefore, it is important to note that although there is not complete congruence in the details of the Islamic finance practice, there are basic principles that are necessary for every Islamic finance contract.

Throughout this book, we will highlight the important elements of each contract. These are elements that must be included or considered when drafting the Islamic finance contract. They are the most basic elements required for any Islamic-compliant contract. The manner in which these elements may be resolved or incorporated differs. The element of good faith should underline every contract. The next section will discuss important elements for any Islamic contract. If you understand and master these principles, you will be able to transfer your knowledge across various Shariah-compliant legal practices.

## Important Elements that are the Underpinnings of Islamic Finance

Islamic finance covers several areas under Shariah law. These basic principles are the underlying foundation providing the necessary building blocks for an understanding of Shariah-compliant contracts. Islamic finance is not an isolated topic in Shariah law. Rather, it is interwoven with other areas of law such as property (tangible and intangible) and contracts. We will briefly discuss each of the various topics to lay the framework for a basic understanding of these laws prior to delving into the various Islamic finance contracts because each of these contracts will have elements rooted into these legal fundamental principles. If these principles are understood, then the reasoning behind certain practices in Islamic finance are more easily understood. Furthermore, understanding these concepts will help you be a more versatile attorney.

# Islamic Legal Concepts of Business Trade

We discussed previously how Islam promotes trade and the development of business relationships within the confines of Islamic law. As we previously indicated, Islam does not separate trading practices or jurisprudence from its religious tenets. Islam is a religion that is all-encompassing. It regulates the personal aspects of an individual's faith as well as describing the manner of practice in the marketplace. Islam is a religion of relationships. It focuses on the development and building of different types of relationships that an individual encounters throughout life. For instance, Islam regulates an individual's relationship with God, her family, and society. The individual's relationship with society is where the laws focus on the marketplace, contractual relationships, and, most pertinent to us, finance principles.

Historically, Islam spread throughout the world via trade and business. It is this regulated relationship of Islam that we will discuss throughout the remaining parts of this book. This is noted because of its mention several times in the primary source, the Quran. Trade is held in high esteem in the Quran.[77] Various passages within the Quran discuss the importance of trade as well as fair dealings associated with these transactions.[78] There are several elements to a basic business transaction that are regulated under Shariah law. The core fundamental elements that Shariah identifies as important are the limits on usury and the concept of fair dealings. These elements are identified as the nature of the business, limits on usury, and fair dealings.

# Contract Law in Islam

Every business transaction involves some type of a negotiation and results in the drafting of an arrangement. Contract law in Islam is derived mainly from the primary source, the Quran. Shariah law has outlined various important elements necessary in a contract. These contractual elements are also necessary in an Islamic finance contract. These elements are very similar to common law contract law principles.

Historically, contract law under Shariah principles was further developed and shaped in the seventh century which, under the Islamic empire, was an agriculturally based society. The marketplace was limited in comparison to today's marketplace. Therefore, you will find that contract law principles in Islam are rudimentary, but scholars use the above-mentioned methodologies to draw further rules and regulations applicable in today's marketplace. The following are basic guidelines necessary in a Shariah-compliant contract. We will first begin with discussing types of contracts, the parties to a contract, and then the important elements necessary to comply with Shaiah contracting principles.

## Types of Contracts

There are three types of contracts in Shariah law: Wa'd (unilateral promise), Muwaaa'adeh (bilateral promise), and Aqd (contract).[79] Shariah law prohibits an individual from entering into two simultaneously binding contracts regarding the same object. Although this may seem unimportant, the type of contract makes a different when drafting the various contracts to enforce specific Islamic finance agreements, such as financing using the Ijara method.

For example, a buyer and seller enter into a rental agreement with a congruent purchase agreement for the same property. If both agreements are drafted as two binding contracts in relation to the same property, this is prohibited in Shariah law and may be unenforceable. However, it is important to note that a promise is not considered to be a contract under Shariah law. Therefore, a bilateral agreement and a separate promise may be entered into in relation to the same property without violating Shariah legal fundamentals.

A promise under Shariah law is considered to be enforceable and an obligation on the party to complete. So a person who promises to undertake an action must attempt in good faith and wholeheartedly to fulfill it. A promise may be unilateral or bilateral. A unilateral promise is one in which one party undertakes an obligation. A bilateral promise is one in which both parties must satisfy specified obligations that are indicated in the contract. Each party must act in good faith to complete the requisite obligations.

An Aqd is considered to be an enforceable binding contract on both parties. In other words, both parties are bound to fulfill the obligations of the contract. It binds both parties simultaneously, whereas a promise does not require both parties to be bound to perform.

It is important to understand these different forms of contracts. Islamic finance agreements take different forms and some transactions utilize several different types of contracts to fulfill the purpose of a financing structure. Therefore, it is common to find an Islamic finance contract that couples a contract (Aqd) with an enforceable promise (Wa'ad) to structure the complete financial deal.

# Parties to a Contract

### Freedom to Contract

Parties have the freedom to contract under Shariah law, just as under common law. Of course, that contract is still bound by what is permissible under Shariah law.[80] For instance, parties may not enter into an illegal contract, such as contracting for the sale of alcohol or drugs, committing murder, or any other impermissible purpose under Shariah law. This principle is equivalent to the fundamental common law contracting principles, which require the subject matter of the contract to be lawful in order for the contract to be enforceable.

### Capacity

There are no restrictions on the type of persons contracting under Shariah law. Shariah law does not distinguish or place restrictions on Muslims and non-Muslims contracting together. Both non-Muslims and Muslims, men and women, have the freedom to contract and enter into business relationships together.[81] A party contracting must have the capacity to contract.[82] Similar to common law provisions, the party must be of an age of majority, coherent, and of sound mind. Those parties prohibited from contracting include minors, mentally incapable individuals, intoxicated persons, and anyone on his or her deathbed.[83] A contract entered into by any of these parties will be deemed void and unenforceable.

As previously noted, although these are the limitations under Shariah law, each jurisdiction may include additional limitations on the parties contracting and their requirements. It is important to understand these limitations prior to drafting a contract, as Shariah law is not the exclusive recognized law within each jurisdiction. Although Shariah law is adopted in many jurisdictions and is highly influential, other laws have also been adopted within those jurisdictions.

### Unconscionability

Another important element in relation to contracting parties is that the contract must be fair. If it is found to be unfair, due to reasons such as imbalance of power in the contract, fraud, misrepresentation, etc., then the contract may be found void and unconscionable. The concern is to maintain the balance in negotiations in the marketplace. A fair marketplace ensures a healthy economy and provides enough opportunity for all to find success. This is an important element that Shariah law seeks to balance.

Therefore, any contract that has traces of fraud, or any other inducements that may disrupt the balance within the marketplace, will be deemed to be void. The Quran continuously seeks to find balance and provide equal opportunity for all.

## Offer, Acceptance, and Consideration

Another important element in a Shariah contract is the concept of offer and acceptance. A Shariah-compliant transaction requires both an offer (Ijab) and acceptance (Qabul).[84] There are several important aspects to this concept under Shariah law.

First, an offer may be made either orally or in writing. Shariah law does not value one over the other or require the offer to be in writing. Of course on an evidentiary level, a written offer is preferable. If an offer and acceptance results in a written contract, the contract is enforceable and binding on the parties. Second, an offer and/or an acceptance may be made directly or via an agent.[85] There are no specific requirements necessary for an offer or acceptance to be in person. Third, offers in writing are deemed to be open until received by the other party.[86] Lastly, consideration is an element of the contract, although it is not required in all jurisdictions. Therefore, it is important to understand this element in relation to the contract that you are drafting and identify the consideration if necessary. If consideration is provided, then it must be in the form of tangible goods, monies, or even an exchange of services.[87] Of course, consideration is limited to those things that are permissible under Shariah law in order to be acceptable.[88]

## Legality of a Contract

We briefly touched on this important element in the above sections. However, it is important to understand because otherwise the contract will be void. As in common law jurisdictions, the subject matter of the contract must be legal and not prohibited under Shariah law.[89] It is important to identify the nature of the activity as well as the transaction itself and any other underlying activities that the company may engage in; otherwise, the contract may be voidable in accordance with Shariah law.[90] For example, when issuing Sukuk (an Islamic bond) of a corporation, the underlying activities of the corporation must comply with Shariah law and may not be prohibited actions.

Shariah law prohibits particular activities. Such activities include engaging in gambling, selling of liquor or pork, pornography, murder, immoral behavior, and profiting from usury. Unless an activity is prescribed as illegal, it is presumed to be lawful. For example the consumption, selling, carrying, and purchasing of alcohol is impermissible under Shariah law. Therefore, a contract to be a liquor distributor would be an impermissible activity and the contract would not be binding, even if all other elements of the contract complied with Shariah law.

This area is most relevant when dealing with corporate transactions. An investigation of the detailed activities of the corporation should be noted and not just a superficial view of the corporation. There should be a due diligence in relation to the activities of the corporation. The due diligence should include a complete analysis of the company's transactions, including any subsidiaries, joint ventures, and so on.

For example, if an Islamic finance transaction included the financing of an airline corporation, a discussion will arise in relation to the selling of alcohol products on the flights and the revenue streams that it generates. That revenue stream under Shariah law is considered to be "unpure." The transaction will fail if that revenue stream is not redistributed outside of the Islamic financial transaction and structure. So, even though the airline industry is in the business of transportation, the secondary revenue stream of alcohol sales will need to be addressed within the scope of the entire transaction. The Islamic contract may not regulate the prohibited activities nor profit from these activities. This is a fundamental nonnegotiable principle.

So an important contracting point to consider is any activity that may be regarded as a detriment to the public health and morals of society. Shariah law governs the underlying nature of the transaction; this principle is not escaped in Islamic finance. Therefore, the nature of any Islamic finance transaction is governed by what Shariah has prohibited and allowed. The lender is not to be indifferent to the activity of the transaction. Rather, the activity is supposed to be part of the entire financing process and not just the lender acting as a facilitator.

## Uncertainty (Gharar)

Another key element to consider when drafting an Islamic contract, whether for a financial transaction or otherwise, is to understand the term Gharar.

Gharar is described as uncertainty or speculative practice in a contract and is forbidden.[2] The literal meaning of Gharar is unknowingly exposing oneself or one's property to jeopardy.[91]

An Islamic contract requires as much certainty and clarity as possible within the transaction to ensure that the terms are clear to all parties involved. Therefore, the contract should define all of the necessary and important elements such as price, quantity, delivery, parties, subject matter, liability, and any other element necessary to maintain clarity between the contracting parties. When the parties ensure that there are no uncertainties or no speculation in the transaction, this maintains an open marketplace and an easy exchange of goods, because few if any obstacles threaten the completion of the transaction.

However, since Gharar is not expressly conveyed in the Quran, it has been left to the Islamic scholars to identify and regulate it. Islamic scholars have divided it into different types of categories.[92] Gharar is defined as being minor, major, and gross in manner.[93] The importance of these distinctions determines the validity of a contract.

A minor Gharar within a contract is acceptable and will not be the reason to invalidate a contract.[94] This type of Gharar is an understanding that there are factors that may not be certain at the time of contracting, but do not constitute a lack of clarity of the major aspects, such as the price or the item that is sold.[95]

An example of a minor Gharar in a contract is insurance (Takaful[3]).[96] The basic premise of insurance is quantifying an uncertainty. The schools of thought disagree with regard to this concept. The Hanbali school of thought prohibits any contract that has uncertainty.[97] However, some scholars of the Hanafi school of thought agree that an insurance contract is permissible.[98] These scholars understand that there are instances where uncertainty is an element in the transaction. An example is the sale of packaged products

---

2.   This term is not readily used in the Quran; rather, the Quran emphasizes the need for clarity between the parties within a transaction. The Quran does mention the concept of prohibiting any injustice and the infliction of harm on any individual in both a physical manner as well as in contracting. One of the Quranic verses states, "O ye who believe, do not squander your wealth illicitly, but let there be amongst you trade by mutual consent and kill not one another. God is ever merciful unto you."[2] Although the word Gharar is not specifically mentioned in this Ayat, the definition is implied. The prohibition of Gharar is mentioned in numerous hadith.[2] Gharar is also referenced and forbidden in the secondary Islamic source of Ijma', the consensus of the jurists.[2]

3.   We will not be discussing Islamic insurance in this book. But, briefly, Takaful insurance is derived from Islamic law and banking principles. It is an insurance with a shared responsibility of liability and is similar conceptually to mutual insurance.

or consumer goods that have natural shells. Although on the outside these products may appear to be good and usable, in practicality they may be spoiled or nonfunctioning. This is the uncertainty part of the contract. A practical example of this is the purchase of a walnut. Walnuts are naturally contained in a hard shell and it is difficult to determine the quality of the nut from examining the exterior. If a seller of walnuts enters into a contract to sell 500 walnuts to a purchaser, it is unlikely that the purchaser will open each walnut to examine it prior to purchase. Therefore, this contract contains a level of uncertainty as to the quality of each walnut received. This minor uncertainty is termed to be Gharar.

Another question is whether, as the size of the contract increases and the level of uncertainty grows, this will also increase the Gharar in the transaction. There is no exact answer to this question; however, it should be noted that minor uncertainties in a contract may be identified and reduced. For example, a bottling company purchases a container of plastic bottles. The uncertainty is how many defective bottles are in each shipment. If the bottler purchases millions of units annually, the level of Gharar in the transaction has just increased at an exponential rate. In order to avoid a concern of Gharar in the transaction, the bottling company and the bottle manufacture may agree on a percentage allowance for each shipment to account for the potential defective goods. This contracting has taken the potential minor Gharar out of the equation of the contract.

Gharar is mostly concerned with specific basic contractual elements and any Gharar arising thereafter would be considered minor. The major elements that constitute Gharar are the following: first, the goods or services that are being contracted need to be in existence; second, the specifics of the product or service are identified and known to both parties; third, the parties need to have dominion and control over the object that is being contracted to ensure its availability for the transaction date; fourth, the termination or date of exchange in the contract should be determined and precise.[99] These are the main contracting elements of any transaction.

The issue of the amount of Gharar in a transaction leads to the question of whether futures may be contracted to in Islam. There are instances during the time of the Prophet Muhammad[4] where Gharar was allowed. These situations balanced the benefit and the potential damages, and it was determined that the benefit outweighed any such potential damages.

A specific instance occurred when the Prophet Mohammad allowed the transaction of the sale of a specific quantity of dates still on the palm tree

---

4.    Peace be upon him.

to take place.[100] Now, how is this defined as Gharar? It is because there is uncertainty as to how many dates were on the palm tree and whether there was a sufficient amount of quality dates to perform the contract. Remember, those are two main elements required in a contract: a verified quantity and the availability of the product to complete the transaction. In this instance, both of these elements were uncertain. Therefore, on the face of this transaction, it should not be allowed. However, it is believed that this transaction was allowed to help cater to those who are less fortunate and to aid the farmers.[101] By allowing such a contract to take place, there is a greater benefit to society and the marketplace than if the transaction were restricted. The date farmer is dependent on selling his crop; however, it is seasonal. So to survive through the remaining months and seasons, he needs to be able to hedge his crop and live on his savings. This is important to understand, because when dealing with Shariah boards and institutions, it may be necessary to explain your legal position as to why or why not a contract should be entered into on an Islamic basis.

Furthermore, the emphasis on limiting the amount of Gharar when contracting is to ensure that the parties to the transaction clearly understand their rights and responsibilities in the contract.[102] An attempt to eliminate Gharar in a transaction is not to eliminate the inherent risk, as risk will always be part of any transaction.[103] However, any potential uncertainty regarding the main issues of contracting is to be eliminated as much as possible in the contract.

There are many practical reasons as to why this is important. First, it helps eliminate any potential misunderstandings that may arise from uncertainty in a contract. This makes clear the duties and responsibilities of all parties in the contract. This also provides easier enforcement of the contract, as it is clear as to who breached and the remedy that should be available. The concept of Gharar is very similar to common law practice. Under the common law jurisdiction, a contract must include specific terms such as price; otherwise, there is no binding contract. If a major Gharar is found in a contract, then the contract is voidable.[104]

In drafting the Islamic contract, make a conscious effort, as in any other contract, to reduce and eliminate any uncertainty, both present and future. This uncertainty includes both parties understanding and having clarity on the subject/object of the agreement, the value of the object, the time of delivery, the price of the object, and any details of future performance. Both parties should seek to reduce the level of uncertainty or unknown in a contract. As the uncertainty diminishes in the contract, a greater level of Shariah compliance is established.

So in practice, it is extremely important to outline the rights and obligations of each party. The contract must state clearly the terms of the agreement such as the object, delivery, price, etc. Uncertainty alone does not constitute Gharar; however, it is important to clearly identify what is possible in the contract. Meanwhile, remember that a commercial contract will always contain minor Gharar, which is acceptable.

## Good Faith

The third important element to any contract under Shariah law is good faith. Every contract must be made in good faith. The Quran highlights the importance of honor and integrity while conducting business--"Honor your contracts."[105] This verse is a brief example of the importance of trade in Islam as well as the importance of fair dealing within a commercial setting.[106] This is similar to common law concepts where bad faith transactions are penalized.

It should also be noted that Islam illegalizes unfair competition. The reason is that unfair competition damages the overall marketplace.[107] The moment that unfair competition enters into a transaction, trust is eroded. Over time, greater disharmony and distrust begin to affect the overall sense in the marketplace. Simple transactions will be more cumbersome, increasing the cost of trade and business transactions. As the cost to trade increases, lower-income individuals will find it difficult to enter into the marketplace, creating a further divide between the socio-economic classes and restricting their opportunities to increase their wealth. Overall, the harm to society will increase and as a result it will affect the economic welfare of the state. It is important to remember that Shariah balances the effects of a transaction on the overall welfare of society and focuses on the effects on weaker members of society. Unfair competition unduly burdens the weaker members of a society.

Also, Shariah law imposes repercussions for engaging in unfair practices. For example, violators will be required to compensate the weaker party for the damages rendered. It is important to understand the enforcement regulations of the jurisdiction and more specifically any special contracting regulation imposed on the stronger party.

## Honesty and Fair Dealings

Another important element in Shariah contract law is commercial honesty and fair dealings.[108] Although it may seem that this is the same as not engaging in fair practices, it is actually different. This is more of an imposition to act in a fair and honest manner.

The Quran specifically reminds merchants not to take advantage of their customers or business associates. Note that the Quran again attempts to protect the weaker members of society. Merchants are obligated to refrain from any dishonest practices and contracts must reflect honesty in order to be enforceable.[109] Merchants are not to exploit consumers or other business partners in order to monopolize the marketplace.[110] The Quran provides examples, such as dishonest practices in measuring goods in the marketplace or using fraudulent weights to defraud customers.[111]

The concept of protecting society and members also includes a prohibition against any deliberate deceptive practice. The Quran explicitly prohibits deceitful practices in several different verses.[112] Such practices include imitation and counterfeiting.[113] The Quran states, "Woe to those who use measure and measure, who when receiving take for themselves a full measure, but when measuring or weighing for others give less!"[114] Many scholars identify that the consumer's interests are of a religious obligation to the marketplace.[115] Some have argued that these verses on a broader scope prohibit all forms of unjust commercial dealing and practices.[116] These scholars further argue that this also includes "deceptive conduct, such as promoting a merchandize by fraudulent means and describing the object differently from its characteristics."[117]

You may be wondering how this applies to Islamic contracts. It can be argued that this concept of "deceptive conduct" may be utilized in the protection of intellectual property. Although this book is focusing on Islamic finance contracts, it is important to understand that Shariah law intersects many different areas and avenues, such as corporate law, intellectual property, property law, and employment law. Furthermore, if you are working in Islamic finance, you need to understand the global reach of Shariah compliance for a financial institution. Therefore, this requires an understanding that deceitful practices are not only elements to be utilized in a financial contract but are also elements in intellectual property infringement cases.

For instance, any infringements on the trademark or logo of a financial institution may have a defense under this concept of not engaging in deceitful practices. Furthermore, anyone who attempts to distribute, promote, or sell the products knowing that the buyer is unaware and participating in an unfair dealing and transaction is also in violation of the Shariah law.[118] Therefore, an important concept in all business transactions should be an understanding of whether the transaction was conducted in a truthful or deceitful nature.

## Trust/Trustee

The concept of a trustee or trust originated at the time of the Prophet Mohammed.[5] Prior to his receiving the revelation, his community had labeled him Al Ameen, "the trusted one." It is this concept, in combination with various passages from the Medjella (from the time of the Ottomans), that confirms the notion of trust within Shariah and verifies that the trustee is entrusted with an asset and holds ultimate responsibility if the asset is damaged or destroyed.[119] The concept of trust is not only important in relation to topics of inheritance, but also in the cases of a financier holding an asset in trust for a borrower. It is important that parties understand their obligations that are both express and implied in the various finance structures that will be discussed in further detail below.

## Usury or Interest (Riba)

Riba is a term that may be defined as usury or interest. This term will provide complexity in the contract that you draft depending on the Shariah board that reviews the contracts and the jurisdiction in which you practice. Unfortunately, there are different perspectives regarding this issue.[120]

Riba is defined as interest. However, this term is unclear among the scholars and carries conflicting positions from various scholars. Some scholars have interpreted Riba to include all forms of interest.[121] This is the strictest interpretation of Riba, which includes simple interest as well as excessive charging of interest.

This theory relies on a fundamental principle that Islam does not view the monetary system as having an intrinsic value; therefore, it cannot generate additional value. Furthermore, the profit or benefit from any transaction is derived from the input of human activity and the production of tangible results. There are also social concerns. The Quran warns that charging interest may be deemed exploitative and lead to injustice and oppression within society. A lot of recent commentary in relation to the global crisis criticizes the lax lending practices that utilized a higher interest rate to hedge risky loans and deals that otherwise would not have been approved.

Other traditions, including Christianity and Judasim, have debated the term of usury within the religious law. The most notable example of this discussion is Shakespeare's play "The Merchant of Venice." Today,

---

5. Peace be Upon Him.

the West defines usury with the words "excessive" or "exorbitant" rate of interest.[122]

A true understanding of economics and a monetary system requires a discussion of interest. Islamic banking rests on the foundation that the interpretation of Riba in the does not include the concept of profit.[123] This distinction gives rise to an allowance of some forms of Riba in order to complete transactions within the realm of Shariah law.

The various forms of Riba include: Riba al-qarud (usury relating to revolving loans) and Riba al-buyu (usury involving trade).[124] Riba al-buyu is further divided into two categories: Riba al-fadl (*simultaneous* exchange of *unequal* qualities or quantities of the same commodity) and Riba al-nisa (*nonsimultaneous* exchange of *equal* qualities or quantities of the same commodity).[125] We will not discuss these in further detail, but they are included to provide you with a greater understanding of the broader concept.

Riba al-qurud is important to understand. This is the accepted and commonly used practice of interest on loans in conventional financing.[126] This practice is also called Riba al-nisia.[127] This type of Riba is described as earning money on money.[128] Riba al-nisia is the conventional understanding of interest, whereby the borrower is charged the predetermined rate of interest in consideration for the monies provided.[129]

Another translation is that the money in the transaction is deferred for payment by adding more money onto the principal in the transaction.[130] For example, compounding interest, annual percentage interest rates, or late fees all increase the principal amount and subsequently the amount due in the transaction by adding the time value of money. This additional amount added onto the loan or borrowing makes it more onerous for the person to repay the debt, thereby altering the balance of power in the contract. This concept is the underlying principle for conventional financing. It is this Riba, which is referenced by Muslim scholars, that is forbidden under Islamic law.[131]

As noted above, some scholars disagree with the absolute prohibition and instead recognize the allowance of a "fair return" and not one that is excessive or burdensome.[132] These scholars reference the practice at which time this prohibition was recognized in Islam.[133] The practice was an excessive charging of interest in which the principal amount would double and in some instances triple due to delays in repayment.[134] This practice clearly violates the underlying business principles in Shariah law by fostering exploitation. Islamic law urges leniency toward debtors and the Quran emphasizes no punishment for unpaid debts.[135] Scholars have further distinguished between "consumption" versus "production" loans or that the prohibition of Riba concerns only individuals and not corporations, banks, or government entities.[136] There are volumes written about the prohibition or the acceptance of various forms of Riba. What is important to note is that the underpinning of Islamic finance is not the prohibition of Riba, but, rather, the acceptance of sharing a profit.[137] If the amount earned can be classified or defined as sharing a profit, than the practice is acceptable under Shariah law.[138] In earning this profit, the lender must be subjected to a partial level of risk in order to truly appreciate the return.[139]

Some interpreters of the Quran have further defined Riba to include any increase in price of a product or contract sought through any "illegal means, such as usury, bribery, profiteering, and fraudulent trading."[140] This is a broader definition of Riba, which is further defined in relation to moral behavior.

So the question arises, how do we handle this in practice? Unfortunately, the solution is not ideal. A lot of the drafting requires finding means and methods to conform an Islamic contract to conventional principles. Most practitioners attempt to bypass the term interest by either relabeling it as a profit or reclassifying the term interest. Ideally, if the contract is reduced to its actual essence, disregarding conventional schemes, the rate of return on the contract should be appropriately calculated and distinguished in the contract. The rate of return is not a prohibited concept in Shariah law; rather, it is encouraged and expected in the marketplace.[141] The bank should bear a risk in entering into the contract and this risk will be counterbalanced by its profit or benefit from the transaction.

When determining the details of the contract, it is extremely important to bear in mind the various factors described above in relation to determining if an element of the contract may constitute Riba (in any form or definition). It is also prudent to complete this exercise when trying to determine the enforceability of such a contract in a Shariah law jurisdiction. Almost all Shariah boards are unanimous in their view that any mention of interest is prohibited. Therefore, it is important to understand the perspective of not only the parties, but also the certifying board to the transaction (if any) in addition to any jurisdictional requirements that may exist.

## Penalty for Late Payments and Other Fees

How does a Shariah contract deal with late payments and fees? Typically, late payment penalties or additional fees are tools used by an institution to recapture additional costs and, in some instances, profit. These fees and penalties must be dealt with carefully as they may be non-Shariah-compliant if they are too excessive. An excessive penalty is one in which the lessor is receiving a profitable consideration. This is deemed noncompliant because earning money on money is considered to be Riba and is forbidden.[142] However, if a penalty is not imposed on a late payment, it will not encourage the lessee to pay timely. Therefore, it is industry practice to use various methods as previously outlined to assist in collecting late payments. These methods include charging a reasonable fee, which does not exceed the costs incurred due to the late payment. For example, the cost of sending out a notice, reasonable follow-up, and the like may be included in the penalty for late payments or fees assessed. The fees assessed for various costs incurred to enter into the transaction are also to be provided at cost and not at an inflated rate, as is sometimes customary in conventional practice. It is important to highlight this point to the parties when drafting the agreements.

For example, Sylvester enters into a financing arrangement with Margot's Bank. Margot's bank typically assesses fees of USD$200 for any late payment. The actual cost that Margot incurs is only USD$50 for any late payment. According to Shariah principles, Margot should only charge her cost of USD$50 for any late payment provided by Sylvester. The USD$150 is non-Shariah compliant. Furthermore, in determining whether to enter into the transaction, Margot's bank required an appraisal and inspection of the property at a total cost of USD$500. Upon entering the contract, Margot's bank may require Sylvester to pay USD$500 as part of the transaction costs. It is important to remember that the owner's costs, such as taxes and homeowner's insurance, may not directly be charged to Sylvester.

The above elements are important in any Islamic contract, including an Islamic finance contract. These are concepts that are easily relatable to common law jurisdictions. We have now laid the foundation and understanding of where Islamic finance originated, what sources are used to determine the regulations, and the basic necessary elements for a contract. The next few sections will discuss property law and then we will discuss in detail current laws, the types of Islamic finance agreements, and key drafting elements.

## Important Elements in Shariah Property Law

Why is it important to understand Shariah property law, when we are interested in Islamic financial structures? Shariah financial structures are based on the concept that the investor (or lender) assumes risk within the transaction. As you will come to note, Islamic finance contracts require the lender to be more than a third party to a transaction. The lender will have to not only take security over the property, but ownership as well. Therefore, it is important when drafting these documents to understand the broader scope of the transaction. Furthermore, the importance of enforcement cannot possibly be stressed enough.

There are several basic elements in Shariah property law that are important. The first important criterion is that the asset must exist. In most contracts, the asset will be required to be in existence at the time of contracting. It is arguable whether the item must be tangible or intangible, but it is agreed that the asset must be in existence.

The second important criterion is that the owner of the property must have title and possession of the asset. The owner must have either physical or constructive ownership of the property. The ownership of the property may not be pending; the owner must have accepted delivery of the asset. For instance, if the transaction involves shares of a corporation, the shares of the corporation must be issued and registered to the individual or corporation prior to entering into the contract. However, this criterion has been challenged and some scholars have noted that this is not a requirement and that an asset may be sold prior to obtaining ownership.[143] The exception to this element is in a Salam or Istisna contract, where the asset is a fungible asset and is a commodity, not something that is unique.[144]

The last important criterion is that the owner must have the right or authority to sell the asset prior to entering into a contract, a basic contracting principle. The person must already possess this right prior to executing a contract for sale. When drafting an agreement relating to an asset, it is important to understand the Shariah board's perspective related to the structure as well as the jurisdictional agreement on this particular point. Otherwise, there will be potential enforcement issues in relation to the contract and its withstanding a strict scrutiny of Shariah property law.

## Where Is Islamic Law Today?

We are now about to delve into the concepts of Islamic finance agreements. We discussed where Shariah law originated and how new regulations are imposed from a religious perspective. But as attorneys, we need to understand how we draft a contract today that can be enforced within the jurisdiction that we are practicing. Furthermore, Shariah requires that Islamic contracts comply with the laws within the jurisdiction in which it is being enforced.

Shariah law has influenced many jurisdictions, predominantly in the Middle East. Those jurisdictions have also adopted their own laws. In most instances, the system adopted was a civil law system. Therefore, although we emphasize the practice of Shariah law in this book, it is important to understand the jurisdictional practices and laws in order to properly draft an enforceable Shariah contract. We focus on the Shariah principles to provide you with the background necessary to understand the important elements in the Shariah contract and how to form these elements in other jurisdictions.

So for a brief understanding, we offer a glimpse of the history of Shariah law and how it became codified. The first codification of Shariah law was under the Ottoman Empire in the form of The Medjella of Legal Provisions in 1865.[145] This legislation may not be considered a primary source of Islamic law, but it is historically significant.[146] The Medjella was developed in congruence with a combination of the Shariah and French statutory law.[147] This commercial code is the first recognized deviation from exclusive Shariah law in the region.[148] It is further important to note that institutional and legal development flourished during this era. After the fall of the Ottoman Empire, a number of Islamic countries relied on the Medjella until they developed their own civil law.[149] As the Ottoman Empire was divided and governed by various Western influences, the legal systems adjusted accordingly.

## What is Islamic Finance?

What is Islamic finance? In its narrowest definition, it is an "asset-based" lending scheme, where one does not collect or pay interest on "rented money" as is done in traditional banking institutions. The Quran specifically admonishes against the practice of "interest" lending. Some scholars differ on the extent of the term "interest," but all agree that egregious interest rates are forbidden. The basic principles in Islamic finance were established by jurisprudence rulings and fatwas, by qualified Muslim scholars. These principles are what generally govern the industry today. There is no one formal set of laws or regulations or jurisdiction under which Islamic finance is practiced. Rather, it is practiced in both eastern and western countries and governed by the laws of those countries. Therefore, it is important to review the terms of any agreement according to the jurisdiction in which it will be enforced. It is further important to review the transaction and ensure the enforceability of the contract within each jurisdiction.

General commercial Shariah-compliant transactions follow a few simple rules when contracting. These include: reaching an agreed upon price without duress; parties are sane and old enough to understand the implications of their actions (Mumayiz); the agreement does not contain uncertainty or deception (Gharar); the goods transacted are in existence under the ownership of the seller; the seller has constructive possession; and the contract is not related to an Islamically forbidden practice. These general rules are the basis of not only Shariah contract law, but of Islamic finance as a whole. You will note that each type of transaction will have traces of each of the above elements.

A cornerstone concept in all Islamic finance transactions is that Riba (usury) is forbidden. One may include a fixed profit and cost amount to a transaction, but not an interest rate. Furthermore, the concept of shared business risk versus a guaranteed return is central for Shariah-compliant financial transactions. These two basic principles distinguish Shariah finance from conventional financing methods and provide stability in the Islamic finance marketplace. Islamic finance is not a market exclusive to Muslims; its stable nature is growing in popularity among non-Muslims globally.

During the current global economic crisis, traditional risk-based securities destabilized the banking and economic centers. Therefore, the markets turned toward alternatives, such as Islamic finance, an area that still experienced growth during the global crisis. The economic growth over the past 30 years in the Cooperation Council for the Arab States in the Gulf (CCASG) and Middle East North Africa (MENA) region was slower than other economies, whose growth was dependent on the private banking industries. Many blame the current global recession on the high-risk financial instruments driven by the private banking sectors. Such high-risk products created immediate wealth and inflation, and subsequently crippled the market during the crash. Conventional products were mainly driven by maximizing the marketplace at any cost while Islamic products are low-risk products meant to maintain long-term financial stability in the marketplace.

The Islamic finance scheme has proven to be stable in the wake of the global financial crisis. Islamic finance was the least affected industry with a reported regional GDP growth of 3 percent in 2009 for the MENA region.[150] The growth in this sector is important to note and provides future opportunities of global growth if properly implemented in accordance with its fundamental principles.

There are many types of Islamic retail products in the marketplace. These products include, but are not limited to, the following types: Murabaha, Mudarabah, Ijara Musharakah, Ijara Mutanaqisa, Tawarruq, Bai Salam, Istisna, and Sukuk. We will review some of these retail products in this book and provide a basic understanding as to how these products function.

# Part III: Types of Islamic Finance Structures

# Types of Islamic Finance Contracts

This section will discuss the various types of Islamic finance contracts that are available. While there are various structural differences in relation to each type of agreement, the same principles generally apply. Therefore, the principles highlighted above which include interest, parties to a contract, Gharar, and good faith interactions all apply to these agreements as well. Note that this is not an exclusive or comprehensive list; rather, these are the most common types of structures and assist in the basic understanding of what Islamic structures generally consist.

## *Murabaha*

The first Shariah-compliant financing structure is the Murabaha, which was used to purchase real assets corresponding to an installment sale contract.[151] Murabaha is typically termed a "cost-plus-profit" financing arrangement.[152] Murabaha is a common short-term contract used in Islamic financing, whereby a financial institution will purchase an asset and sell the asset to the ultimate buyer at a disclosed profit. Murabaha is used in various types of agreements such as those that include property, microfinance, commodities, and trade. Conventionally, a Murabaha may be translated as a buy-sell back arrangement. This contract has two basic promises: the first is a promise from the customer that he will purchase the asset from the bank. The second is a promise from the bank that it will, in fact, sell the customer that asset, after acquisition.[153] This particular transaction requires the buyer to know the price at which the bank will purchase the asset as well as the profit earned by the bank to complete the transaction.[154]

What is the process? The process is simple. The bank purchases the asset and becomes its full legal owner, assuming all ownership risks. After this purchase, the bank adds a calculated profit to the sale price.[155] The profit added is the lender's reward for the risk taken in the purchase, especially since the bank will bear the burden of the asset's resale to the customer as a true owner.[156] This is an interesting distinction from other Islamic finance products that require the financier to bear the burden of risk in a transaction. In this specific type of a transaction, the financier does not bear any risk other than the interim ownership risk. The selling price then is a fixed price with a fixed schedule of payments or a one-time payment, depending on the contractual agreement with the customer.[157] Since it is an asset-backed financing scheme, it requires a commodity in order to be valid under Shariah law.

An example of this agreement is Henry Homebuyer who wants to purchase a home in Illinois. Henry approaches Billy's bank to finance the deal. Billy's bank conducts a due diligence on the property, assessing the risk of ownership, Henry's qualifications, the fair market value of the property, and the purchase price. Billy's bank then decides to offer a Murabaha arrangement for the transaction. Henry agrees. Billy's bank agrees with Henry that Billy's bank will purchase the home at a price of USD$250,000 from Steve Seller. After acquiring title and possession to the property, Billy's bank agrees to sell the home to Henry Homeowner at a price of USD$322,000 with specified monthly payments for a term of 15 years. Henry Homeowner and Billy's bank agree to the terms. Billy's bank then purchases the home on behalf of Henry Homeowner at the agreed upon price of USD$250,000. Billy's bank then resells the home to Henry the Homeowner at the agreed upon greater price of USD $322,000 over the course of 15 years. There are several key elements to note regarding a Murabaha contract that will be discussed in the following section.

# Important Elements Necessary in Murabaha Financing

It is important to remember the elements regarding Shariah contracts previously discussed. The following sections will reiterate important elements relating to Murabaha financing and ways to ensure compliance with Shariah principles and in accordance with a Murabaha structure.

## Asset

A Murabaha contract is an asset-based contract. Therefore, it is important that the Shariah guidelines imposed on property and ownership are followed. The Murabaha transaction requires the transference of an asset from the seller to the bank and then to the ultimate customer. First and foremost, the asset is to be in existence at the time of contracting. This is a basic principle to be adhered to under Shariah. For example, a Murabaha agreement may not pertain to a good that has yet to be manufactured. Typically, the asset is manufactured and available for immediate resale.

Second, title and ownership of the asset must be held by each entity that sells the asset. Therefore, the financier may not sell the asset without properly holding title prior to the transfer.[158] Remember, under Shariah, in order for the financier to have the right to sell the asset, the financier must own the asset being sold.

For example: Leila approaches Philips Finance to purchase computers for retail sale. Leila has just opened her business and does not have enough cash to finance the initial purchase of computers. Philips Finance agrees to purchase the computers at an agreed upon mark-up in price and provides Leila six months to repay the debt. Leila agrees to the terms. Philips Finance enters into an agreement with the computer manufacturer to purchase the computers for Leila. After the agreement is signed and Philips Finance has either taken possession or title of the computers, Philips Finance enters into an agreement with Leila to sell her the computers at the agreed upon terms. Leila than takes possession of the computers and sells them on the market. The fundamental principle underlying this element is that if there is no asset that is being sold or transacted, the transaction is based on a currency transaction exclusively, which is contrary to Shariah principles.

If the property is not properly transferred to the financing institution, this will be a point of concern at the time enforcement of the agreement is required. Furthermore, the title to the goods does not completely transfer without the full payment received by the financier. Many institutions in practice disregard the element of title and have faced difficulty in enforcing the Islamic contract.

There is a form of a Murabaha structure that we will not delve into in this book that includes the concept of an Istisna structure. Istisna is literally tanslated as "let one build" in Arabic.[159] This allows the financing of a new home or an item that is to be built. However, in order to ensure a foundation of understanding of Shariah-compliant concepts, it is important under a Murabaha that the above elements of an asset are adhered to when contracting between parties.

## *Ownership/Risk*

When the lender initially purchases the asset, there must be a full transfer of the asset to the lender. The lender must be a true owner bearing all the risk that is typically associated with owning an asset until resale.[160] The lender will be responsible for any damage, risk, or loss.[161] For example, Baber Borrower asks Fahad Finance to purchase on its behalf vases and sell them to Baber Borrower at a profit with installment payments. Fahad Finance purchases the vases from Mills Manufacturing and has them shipped to Baber Borrower's warehouse. Fahad Finance retains title over the vases as they are shipped in Fahad Finance's name to the warehouse. Mills Manufacturing ships the vases F.O.B. to Mills' warehouse. Unfortunately, as the vases are being shipped from Mills' warehouse, a few cases are damaged on the truck. Legally, the cases belong to Fahad Finance. Therefore, Baber Borrower is not obligated to pay for any of the losses incurred, since the vases belong to Fahad Finance.

It should be noted that in the resale, the lender will also warrant the asset to the customer as a true owner of the asset. The resale may not occur until the financier has title of the commodity. Based on our above example in the resale to Baber Borrower, the cost of those vases may not be included and Fahad Finance must warrant the remaining vases that are sold to Baber Borrower at a profit. The lender also assumes the risk that the customer may elect to not purchase the asset. Following the same example above, Fahad Finance runs the risk that Baber Borrower will elect not to purchase the vases. In that event, Fahad Finance is responsible for the vases and may also be responsible for finding an alternative buyer.

There are various opinions regarding a Murabaha agreement. The most notable is the concern that it does not represent or reflect a loan agreement. Therefore, ensuring that ownership is properly transferred is extremely important. Otherwise, the transaction may be deemed a conventional loan and not an arrangement in accordance with Shariah.

### Price and Payment

Another important element to consider in a Murabaha transaction is the price. There are actually two separate parts to a Murabaha transaction.[162] The first part of the transaction entails the initial purchase by the financier of the product from the supplier on behalf of the borrower. In this initial part of the transaction, the price is determined between the financier and the supplier. As must occur under any Shariah-compliant transaction, the price must be clearly identified between the parties.[163]

In the second part of the transaction, the price must also be clearly identified between the parties. It should be noted that the price in the second part of the transaction includes a profit.[164] The profit margin is disclosed to the buyer.[165] Unlike conventional financing, the mark-up in the price by the financier is for the actual services rendered by the financier.[166] If the bank purchased the asset at a different price than that which is listed in the contract with the customer, the customer has the option to void the contract.[167]

This is not intended to be a financing transaction. Rather, it is intended to be a marketplace sale. However, the price may be paid in installments over a period of time.[168] There is no specificity as to the length of time over which the price may be paid. However, typically this is a short-term contract between the parties. The same elements about late payments and penalties and fees under Shariah contracts apply under this instance as well.[169] Fees attributed to the transaction may be added, but are to be added at the actual cost incurred and not used as an income-generating mechanism.

A Murabaha agreement is typically a commodity-based transaction and not to be used if there are other means to achieve the desired transactional result. Each transaction is considered to be a separate and independent transaction. The Murabaha mirrors daily transactions found in the marketplace whereby a middle merchant helps move goods into the marketplace for a profit.

## Types of Contracts Used in a Murabaha Structure

In a commodities Murabaha transaction, the contracts typically used include a master agency agreement and a master Murabaha agreement.

In a Murabaha financing with an asset such as a vehicle, the typical contracts include: Murabaha financing agreement, Murabaha sale contract, promise to purchase, purchase order, and a delivery order. The combination of these contracts outlines the transaction in a manner that does not contradict the Shariah. It is important to note that the promise to purchase is not a contract, but rather, as previously discussed, it is a promise to not conflict with the Shariah principles of contracting.

### *Tawarruq[6]*

Tawarruq is a derivative of a Murabaha transaction, which is also referred to as a reverse Murabaha agreement.[170] Tawarruq is a type of arrangement that allows the financing institution to bind the customer with one contract, thereby reducing the bank's risk.[171] In essence, the financier purchases the goods directly from the seller and enters into a payment plan with the buyer.[172] The buyer also sells the goods at a loss and pays the loan from the bank in installments.[173] The most prevalent example of such a transaction is in in business. For example, David Distributor finds beautiful silk scarves that he wants to purchase from Sally Silk. Sally requires full payment of the scarves prior to shipment. David Distributor is just starting his business and needs financial assistance to procure the scarves. In the interim, David has already found a buyer for the scarves, Barbara Beautician. Barbara has agreed to have the scarves shipped to her directly and she will pay David cash upon delivery. This arrangement is considered Tawarruq as the sale bypasses the distributor and neither the financial institution nor the first buyer take actual ownership or possession of the goods. There is an

---

6.   We will not discuss Tawarruq in detail. It should be noted that this is a transaction that is not favorably viewed by pious Muslims who argue such a transaction is an attempt to implement conventional practice under the guise of Shariah finance.

inherent risk in this transaction, because if either portion of the transaction is unknot completed, then the ownership of the asset may be in question and a point of contention.[174]

In the above instance, the financier purchases the goods, sells them to the distributor on a payment plan option, and the distributor sells the goods to a final end user. There are several Shariah concerns regarding this type of transaction. The most important concern is that the scarves are not properly transferred between the buyers. As previously indicated, the seller must own the asset in order to have the right to sell it...

Overall, Tawarruq transactions are highly criticized in the financial industry. Tawarruq transactions add debt into the marketplace. Under Shariah economics, debt is frowned on and not the means by which to stimulate the marketplace. Furthermore, the concern regarding Tawarruq is the overpricing of the commodity to the marketplace and the fact that the price paid for the commodity increases and becomes greater than the value of the good. There is no positive wealth that is added back to society; rather, there is an increase in liability in the marketplace.[7] Many argue that the benefits of a Tawarruq arrangement outweigh the negatives and therefore should only be used as a mode of financing in extreme situations. A Tawarruq arrangement is usually entered into by a borrower that is in need of liquidity.[175]

It is extremely important to note that some jurisdictions do not accept a Tawarruq transaction and find it Islamically impermissible. Therefore, prior to drafting any documents or reviewing a transaction, it is important to confirm that the transaction is permissible and enforceable in the applicable jurisdiction. It is further important to confirm with the financial institution that such a transaction is permissible in accordance with its Shariah advisory board.

## Important Elements Necessary in Tawarruq Financing

If a Tawarruq transaction is acceptable (as noted above). then it is important to note the elements below in order to ensure compliance.

---

7.   This is a fundamentally important point as the current global crisis is blamed on the overcreation of debt in the marketplace that was displaced from the initial assets funded. Many papers have been written about this topic. It is important to point out that Islamic economics are conscious about the creation of debt and disdain the separation of debt from the asset in the marketplace.

*Asset*

Under Shariah law, it is important that the finance transaction continue to maintain a close connection to the asset. Due to the nature of a Tawarruq transaction, there is a possibility that the true market value of the asset will be less than the amount that it is being sold into the marketplace.

It is also important to rehighlight the point discussed above relating to the ownership of the asset. Due to the nature of the transaction, in the event that there is a portion of the transaction that is incomplete, the ownership of the asset may be in question and a point of contention between the parties.[176] Most Shariah boards require the transfer of ownership to be clear in order to avoid this particular concern, which is further discussed below in Ownership Risks.

*Ownership Risks*

Another concern in a Tawarruq transaction is that title will not properly transfer throughout the transaction. It is important that the title of the assets transfers properly in order to comply with Shariah. As for ownership, the consequences of ownership will be borne by the party that owns legal title of the asset, regardless of whether the overall transaction is not complete, or whether a party is acting as an agent during the interim transaction. In the end, the same ownership risks apply in a Tawarruq transaction as apply in the Murabaha transaction.

*Price and Payment*

Since Tawarruq is a derivative of a Murabaha, the transaction is very similar. The difference between the types of transactions is that the cost of a Murabaha is greater than that of a Tawarruq. A Murabaha has two sets of closing costs: the first is the initial transaction between the supplier and the financier and the second is between the financier and the buyer. The closing costs include any transfer of title, shipment costs, representation costs, escrow, etc. Inevitably, these costs are built into the purchase price, thereby increasing the cost of a Murabaha transaction.

In a Tawarruq transaction, the costs are condensed. The reason is that there is only one overall transaction between the parties.[177] The financier purchases directly from the seller and sells it to the buyer in one transaction.[178] Typically, the product does not exchange hands or title and the transaction is fairly seamless.

## Ijara

There are two main types of an Ijara agreement. In the most common definition, Ijara is defined as leasing.[179] The first type is a standard landlord-tenant relationship in which the landlord owns a property and leases it to the tenant for a specified price and period of time. This type of an Ijara uses a standard lease agreement signed between the parties. There are specific lease obligations and rights that are to be considered, but there is nothing too varied from a conventional perspective in this type of an agreement.

The second type of an arrangement is the use of an Ijara contract as a financing vehicle. This also can take multiple forms in that it may be relevant to an asset under construction or a constructed asset that a borrower is looking to finance. This arrangement is similar to a lease with an option to buy; however, the agreements are not as simple as the transactions under Shariah law and require separate agreements.[8]

An Ijara arrangement includes a "transfer of ownership of a service for a specified period of time for an agreed upon lawful consideration."[180] Ijara is most commonly used as an alternative to conventional mortgage contracts. In this type of contract, the financial institution will purchase the equipment or building and lease the asset to the buyer at an agreed upon price.[181] The installment payments are equal to the value of the asset. At the end of the installment agreement, the lessee will be the owner of the asset or the asset is returned to the financier. Both types of agreements require basic elements to the contract.

A financed structure under an Ijara agreement utilizes the following agreements. First, the financier enters into a sale and purchase agreement with the current property owner. The financier purchases the property and places title to the property in the financier's name. The financier and the borrower enter into a lease agreement. The borrower and financier enter into a sale undertaking and a purchase undertaking. These latter agreements are used as a promise that in the future the borrower will purchase the asset. Remember, there are limitations under Shariah as to the types of agreements one can enter into regarding the same asset. For further clarification on this structure, refer to the Appendix.

---

8.  There are limitations to agreements and promises under Shariah law. Refer to the section regarding types of contracts.

# Basic Elements to an Ijara Contract

There are several basic elements that must be considered in any Ijara relationship. These elements include the value of the asset, ownership, obligations of the parties, liabilities of the parties, and the use of the property. Further, it is important to identify the long-term nature of the contract: will it be a financing arrangement or exclusively a rental agreement? It is also critical to review the structure under each specific jurisdiction and identify any additional risks or obligations for the parties. Also, determine if there are any additional fees or costs that are to be considered based on the agreements. These categories outline the basic structure of an Ijara agreement.

## Asset

First, for Shariah purposes, it is important to ensure that the object being leased is clearly identified in the contract. The asset may be described in the contract by location, type, property identification number, or any other description that may clearly identify it. The asset that is subject to the Ijara is not required to be real property; however, it must be clearly identifiable. For example, if the property was a piece of machinery, then the contract will specify the serial number on the machine, the make and model, and any other descriptive details to identify that this particular machine is the asset governed by the Ijara contract.

A second important element is that the asset must have an inherent sustainable value. If the asset has no value, then it may not be leased. The underlying concept of an Ijara is that an asset is exchanged for consideration. For there to be consideration, there must be value to the asset and it must have a valuable use. In order to clarify this point further let's review an example. George seeks to finance the purchase of an apple. The apple in the marketplace has an inherent value of USD$1. The apple is a perishable and consumable product and, therefore, although it has a marketplace value, the apple may not be financed. The value of the apple is consistently diminishing as it is slowly rotting or, if the apple is consumed, its inherent value ceases to exist. Therefore, the apple is not an appropriate asset under an Ijara financing arrangement. The value and usability of the asset must be known to both parties in the transaction for it to be compliant. This requires disclosure of any defects in the asset that are known to the parties at the time of contracting. Any defects will affect the value of the asset and is relevant to the fairness of the entire contract.

Third, the asset being leased must be lawful under Shariah law and under the jurisdiction where the agreement is taking place. For example, equipment used to manufacture illegal drugs may not be financed using an Ijara agreement. Also, although in some jurisdictions the manufacturing of alcohol is permissible, it is impermissible under Shariah. Therefore, although the equipment may be financed, it may not be financed using Ijara financing.

The fourth element relating to the asset is that it must be deliverable. As noted, Ijara is used as a method of financing. In some instances, Ijara is used to finance the purchase of properties under construction, which makes this particular element important. The asset does not need to be in existence as long as it may be described in particularity and detail. This is to avoid any confusion or later dissonance between the parties and the asset. Therefore, Ijara financing may be used to finance properties under construction... In the event that the asset is not currently available, it must be deliverable by the future date as indicated in the contract. For example, the asset requires nine months of construction... The future date of the contract may not be less than nine months.

## Ownership Rights

Whether an agreement is a basic lease or a lease-to-purchase agreement, during the time of "rental" the owner of the property must remain the lessor.[182] This is a crucial element and in many instances overlooked. This limits the secondary marketplace under Islamic financing which is common to conventional financing.

When a financier is entering into the transaction, according to Shariah principles the financier must take ownership of the title to the property. The title will not be transferred to the borrower until the termination of the rental period and the sale and purchase undertakings are invoked. The rental of the asset does not transfer any ownership rights to the lessee by any means.[183] The lease agreement is a typical lease agreement whereby exclusive usage rights to the asset are allowed. Only the use of the asset is transferred to the lessee. As typical under any standard lease agreement, the lessee is given the right to use the asset during the term of the lease in consideration for the rental payments.[184] Using the same example from above, an apple may not be leased under an Ijara agreement, because once the apple is used, the ownership transfers from the original owner to the user.

Since the ownership rights are maintained with the financier, the financier is subject to obligations and liabilities as the legal owner of the asset during this interim financing period. There are also obligations and liabilities on behalf of the borrower, who is acting as a tenant during this interim period. The next section will briefly discuss each of these rights.

## Obligations and Liabilities of the Parties

The obligations and liabilities of the parties to an Ijara contract are the same in both types of Ijara structures. It is important to ensure that, contractually, these elements are reflected in the transaction documents. Also, it is important to review the enforceability of each of the different elements within the practicing jurisdiction as there may be specific elements that require further attention or consideration. First, let us take a look at the lessee.

### Lessee

The lessee cannot use the leased asset for any purpose other than what is explicitly designated in the contract. If it does so, the lessee will be in breach of the contract. If the contract does not explicitly state the purpose for which the asset will be used, then the asset is presumed to be used for its common purpose (e.g., a house to live in or a car to drive). For instance, Selma and ABC Finance enter into an Ijara structure for a single family home to be used for an in-home business purpose. Selma discusses her ambition to start a hair salon in her home with ABC Finance. ABC Finance purchases the property and enters into a lease arrangement with Selma. Selma moves her equipment into the home and lawfully begins her business. In the event that the contract does not clearly stipulate the purpose for which the asset will be used, it will be presumed that Selma will be using the asset for her personal use and not for operating a business. In this particular instance, Selma will be in breach of the lease agreement.[9]

It must be noted that if the lessee uses the asset for any uncommon use or without authorization from the lessor, the lessee is subject to any liability from that unauthorized use. This is also a jurisdictional issue as it is closely intertwined with dispute resolution and potential litigation.

---

9.   This scenario does not consider any litigation arguments or potential evidence used to argue on behalf of either party. Nor does it reflect how a jurisdiction will rule on this scenario. This scenario is just to highlight the relevant point.

The lessee is also under an obligation to pay for all "wear and tear" on the asset upon entering into a security agency agreement. This agreement transfers the liability, which is typically held by an owner, and places it on the lessee. This is a standard element in any conventional lease, whereby the lessee is liable for all maintenance payments and usage payments associated with the asset. For example, Charlie's Chips, a potato chip manufacturer, is financing the chip manufacturing machinery from Funky Financier. Charlie has several pieces of equipment that are used regularly in the chip-making process. These machines are currently financed under an Ijara structure from Funky Financier. The potato chip making machinery requires weekly maintenance and, occasionally, costly replacement parts are needed. The weekly maintenance, replacement parts, and any installation costs to be paid are the responsibility of Charlie's Chips. Charlie's Chips needs to replace and maintain the machines as closely as possible to retain the same market value for Funky Financier.

## Lessor

The lessor also has obligations and liabilities, even though the lessor is working as a temporary intermediary in this financing process. The lessor is the legal title owner of the property. The lessor should disclose the asset on its balance sheet and in its asset portfolio. This is an important element and often overlooked in various jurisdictions. But for all intents and purposes, the asset belongs to the lessor during the term of the lease, regardless of any future transactions.

Therefore, the lessor is obligated to pay any costs of the asset that are not attributable to use and are considered ownership costs.[185] Such costs include, but are not limited to, annual taxes, homeowners' insurance, homeowner association fees, registration of title, and any other service charges or "owner" charges with regard to the asset. As indicated above, the lessee will only be responsible for maintenance or usage costs, such as regular maintenance, if a security agency agreement is entered into between the parties. Otherwise, the lessor bears this responsibility as the owner of the property.[186] If, for example, this were an apartment that was to be financed, the lessee would be required to pay for maintenance costs, such as a dishwasher requiring replacement, or the cost to unclog a drain.

It is important to note that if the asset is no longer usable, the Ijara contract is immediately terminated as the Ijara contract is based on the asset itself. There are specific points to consider in this regard. The first point is if the asset is no longer able to be used due to negligence of the lessee, than the lessee is responsible for the loss and must compensate the lessor for the market value of the asset prior to the loss. For instance, John has entered into an Ijara agreement for a single family home with Frank's Finance. On behalf of John, Frank's Finance has purchased the home from the developer and is providing a lease agreement to John over the course of the next 25 years at which time John has entered into a purchase undertaking with Frank's Finance to purchase the property at the end of the lease. In this instance, John has taken possession of the property. The property is still legally owned by Frank's Finance. John has a Fourth of July party and a friend accidentally leaves a cigarette burning, causing the curtains to catch fire and destroying the house. In this instance, as would be the same under any lease, John is liable for the negligence of his friend and would have to pay the market value for the home at the date prior to the incident.

The second scenario is a bit different. If, in this case, on the Fourth of July a random firework from a public fireworks display lands on the roof causing a spark which completely destroys the home, this is not John's responsibility. The home was not destroyed due to his negligence and he will not be liable to replace the home. Therefore, if the asset is lost or destroyed due to circumstances outside the control of the lessee, than the lease is terminated and the lessor bears the burden of the loss. In order to protect from any loss, the lessor may elect to insure the property using the Islamic mode of Takaful. This is typically at the expense of the lessor and is typically stated in the Ijara contract.

When the financial institution is reviewing the project, it is to consider all the various risk factors of the project and the costs associated with them. In some instances, financial institutions may not be conscious of all the costs, such as the cost of transferring title from the developer to the financier and then from the financier to the individual. This is a double cost and is in many instances overlooked. Regardless, it is important that the financier consider all of these obligations and risks when determining the rental payments and terms of the contract.

## Rental Payments

Rental payments are a key element in any leasing agreement, including an Ijara contract. There are several points to consider when outlining rental payment obligations in an Ijara transaction. It is important to note a fundamental difference between a conventional contract and a Shariah-compliant contract in this regard. Under a conventional contract, the payment obligations may begin immediately. However, under a Shariah-compliant contract, such an arrangement is unacceptable unless the asset has been provided to the lessee.[187]

First, the rental payment amount must be clearly specified in the contract and identifiable to the parties involved. This avoids Gharar in the transaction. The underlying rationale is to promote transparency in the transaction between the parties and allow each party to identify his or her own level of risk. Generally, rental amounts are the same over the course of the contract and do not fluctuate. However, there is no limitation on the manner in which the rental payment is defined as long as it is clear to the parties. Therefore, the lessor may vary the rental payments over the term of the contract.

For example, Tim is renting an apartment to Adam for USD$1,000 per month for a term of five years. The contract states that the rental payments are subject to a 10 percent annual increase each year. This is acceptable under an Ijara contract. What happens if we modify the above example to the following? After an annual review, Tim reserves the right to modify the rental payments as desired during the course of a five-year term. Under this example, the terms of the contract are unacceptable under Shariah standards. The lessee, Adam, is unable to determine accurately his risk and obligations under this transaction. Therefore, the transaction is deemed to have too much uncertainty and is unacceptable under Shariah standards.

However, it is important to note that the financial institution will still be able to modify the rental payments and take into account market pricing, as long as it is clearly stated and identifiable within the contractual arrangement. Outlining such details in a contract would include identifying the various rental periods and the structure of the payments and any adjustments that would be undertaken at each adjustment period. The important element to note is that the individual incurring the payment of the financial obligation needs to understand how the payments will be calculated. Although interest is not an element of a Shariah contract, in practice various financial institutions practicing in the Islamic finance sector will impose a base rate that is published and adjust the rental payments accordingly at each specified rental period. This is a prime example of the way Islamic finance in practice has adopted conventional aspects.

The second important point is time limit. Under an Ijara arrangement, there is no designated time limit with regard to rental payments. Rental payments are not required to be in fixed increments of 30 days or for a term of 30 years. This is a contractual arrangement between the parties and negotiated accordingly. As in any conventional contractual relationship, the lessor may shorten or lengthen the time periods to allow for a renegotiation of terms if it is exclusively a lease agreement or lengthen the time period to accommodate a financing structure. The lease period and terms related to rental payments should be clearly identified in the contract in order to have transparency in relation to the liabilities involved. This is necessary to avoid any Gharar in the transaction.

In the event that the Ijara is exclusively a lease agreement and the lease period is shortened (e.g., to one year) to allow for renegotiation and an agreement between the parties is not reached while the lessee is occupying the premises, then the lessee must vacate the premises and the lessor has an option to find a new tenant. For example, Sasha owns an apartment and is currently leasing this apartment to Adam. The rental period in the simple Ijara contract is for six months, at which time the terms of the agreement may be renegotiated. During the six months, the property taxes in the area rise significantly. So Sasha seeks to increase the rental payments from USD$2,200 to USD$2,500 per month. Adam refuses the increase as his budget only allows him an increase of USD $2,350. Sasha and Adam are unable to find a common agreement and elect not to renew the Ijara contract. As such, Adam should vacate the premises and Sasha is free to find a new tenant at the new price.

The above scenario illustrates what should happen if an agreement between the parties is not reached upon renewing an Ijara agreement. The lessee vacates the premises and the lessor has the option of finding a new tenant. Of course, this is an easy solution in a basic lease relationship. The underlying principle is that the parties to the transaction must agree to the basic principles and terms of the contract. These terms must be identifiable to both parties to assess their individual risk in entering into the contract.

When a financial institution is pricing the rental payments under an Ijara financing arrangement, there are certain considerations regarding the profit to be made. It is understood that an algorithm is used to identify the inflation and long-term profits to be made on each transaction. In some instances, financial institutions seeking to provide Islamic financing would like to use a benchmark that reflects the changes in the marketplace over the course of the long-term Ijara agreement. In order to use a benchmark that adjusts periodically and still provide transparency in the contractual arrangement, shorter time periods allowing for readjustment of the rental payment within a specified range may be utilized. Although this is not an approved practice among all scholars, some scholars are allowing such an agreement to proceed as Shariah-compliant.

How does this work? Farouk is seeking Ijara financing to purchase a property in Istanbul. He approaches Shariah Finance for financing. Shariah Finance agrees to enter into an Ijara financing structure whereby Shariah Finance will purchase the property and lease it to Farouk. The rental payments will be due every 30 days with quarterly rental periods benchmarked at the Shariah Finance rate. The rental payment will be the published Shariah Finance rate plus 1 percent and the base rate is not to exceed a fluctuation of 2 percent.

Although, some scholars have allowed such terms as Shariah-compliant, others view these terms as a guise to implement conventional financing as Islamic financing. The scholars in favor of these structures argue that this is exclusively a benchmark to help determine the rental and that such benchmark is not the only source used for determination. Those opposed to this reiterate that the rental payments are still ambiguous and unfair to the lessee and, therefore, invalid under Islamic financing principles. The counter to this statement is that the parties are mutually agreeing to the use of the benchmark. The benchmark is clearly defined and the parties have the right to freedom of contract.

The second argument against the use of a benchmark is that there is an unforeseen loss to both of the parties in the event that the benchmark suddenly fluctuates in either direction. As a result, in most contracts the benchmark may be qualified with a high and/or low cap. For example, a benchmark may be set as, "no greater than 15 percent and no less than 5 percent." Lastly, there is an argument to be made that unlike conventional financing, the lessor is not entitled to interest regardless of the benefit to the lessee. In an Ijara contract, the lessor assumes the risk of the leased asset even though the lessor does not have possession. When drafting the agreement, it is important to highlight these risks and arguments to the parties involved. Also, it is to be noted that the Shariah board reviewing the contract may object to such terms.

An interesting point to consider is that rental payments may be collected prior to the asset being in possession of the lessee. However, this is contingent that the monies collected are considered "on account" payment from the lessee. This payment can also be classified as a security deposit. It must be noted that this security deposit payment needs to be adjusted against the rent. Therefore, the contract is to include appropriate provisions designating a security deposit as rental payments and adjusting these payments against the rent.

If an Ijara contract has a future date of delivery, then the rental payments should not begin until the delivery of the asset to the lessee. But for practical purposes, this is sometimes overlooked in Islamic financing, even though it is contrary to Shariah principles. It is usually bypassed by creative uses of the security deposit payments that begin at the time of the purchase. An example of an Ijara contract as a financing vehicle is the following: The bank purchases the property from the developer. The title of the property transfers to the bank after the purchase. The bank meanwhile enters into an Ijara contract (lease to purchase) with the lessee, where the contract stipulates payments beginning on the date of purchase by the bank. The property does not transfer until it is available and is not linked to or contingent on the payment schedule. Practically, the bank is attempting to ensure its risk by purchasing the property on behalf of the lessee from the developer. It is important to note that in this type of arrangement, the financier bears the burden in the event that the developer does not deliver the asset, because it is the financier that is the true owner of the asset.

## Late Rental Payments

A penalty on late rental payments is prohibited under Shariah, unlike conventional contracts. However, by not including a clause in the arrangement between the parties, there is no incentive for the lessee to pay on time, which increases the financing risk of delayed payments. There are several ways that an Ijara agreement can deal with such a concept. These include, but are not limited to, a donation clause, acceleration, or termination of the contract.[188]

As previously discussed, Ijara in its true form is a lease agreement; however, many financial institutions implementing Islamic finance use the Ijara agreement as a financing vehicle. Although this has become a common financing method, there are underlying elements to this that are non-Shariah-compliant, but still are implemented, such as rental payments, even when there is a delay in delivery of the asset. Remember, under Shariah principles, payments on the rental of an asset are not to begin until the delivery of the asset. The reason Shariah does not favor payment obligations on the lessee to begin prior to the property transfer is that there is no consideration for those payments. The payments in essence are payments in consideration for the money that was forwarded by the bank. So these payments are similar to that of interest and earning money on money is forbidden under Islamic law.[189] The ideal Shariah method for this transaction is that the rental payments commence after the property is transferred to the lessee.

## Subleasing and Assignment of an Ijara Contract

First, let's review a sublease and whether it is permissible. A sublease is typically impermissible unless it is clearly provided for in the contract and done with the permission of the lessor. This is based on the important principle of allowing the parties the freedom to contract. The permission of the lessor is required, because the lessor has the right to contract with whom he or she desires. This same rationale is used to limit the assignment of the contract by the financing institution to the secondary marketplace without the authorization of the lessee. The lessee has the right to determine with whom he is contracting, the terms of the agreement, etc.

For instance, Haifa has entered into an Ijara financing agreement for a warehouse with Mustapha Bank. The Ijara agreement contains a provision allowing Haifa to sublease the warehouse space with the permission of Mustapha Bank. Due to a downturn in the economy, Haifa is unable to continue to afford the payments on the warehouse and is seeking to reduce her inventory and tighten her balance sheet. Among the solutions Haifa considers is subleasing the warehouse until the market picks up again. Haifa knows that her friend, Ali, is looking for a place to store his goods. She offers Ali the space.

In a conventional marketplace, the loan is typically sold to a secondary market and the terms of the agreement may vary upon notice. Under Shariah law, such a system is unacceptable as the freedom to contract between the parties is hindered. The lessee becomes the weaker party, losing bargaining power and balance in the contract. These are all principles contrary to Shariah guidelines.

Can a lessee subleasing a property profit from the new sublease? The different schools of thought under Shariah vary in their views regarding a lessee's right to profit from a sublease. Some state that it is acceptable and others state that any profit earned on a sublease is impermissible. The Quran and the Sunna do not officially rule on this so it is up to the individual interpretation, the interpretation of the Islamic financial institution, and any jurisdictional limitations. Using the above example, Haifa may sublease the property to Ali with the permission of Mustapha Bank. Depending on the jurisdiction and Haifa's personal practices, she may sublease the warehouse at a profit or at the same price that she is paying to Mustapha Bank.

Similarly, the assignment of the rental payments requires the permission of the parties and should be provided for in the Ijara contract. Profiting on the assignment of rental payments is questionable. The profit earned on such an assignment would be considered earning money from money (as you recall, a forbidden practice). However, if the party earning the assigned rentals was a partial owner, or there were costs to transfer the monies, then these costs would be acceptable and may be provided for in the contract.

## Termination of the Ijara Contract

How does an Ijara contract terminate? Shariah forbids the unilateral termination of an Ijara contract if both parties are upholding the terms of the agreement. Therefore, a financial institution may not unilaterally terminate the contract if the lessee is making timely payments. This is to protect the lessee for fulfilling his or her contractual obligations. However, if the lessee has defaulted, the financial institution may unilaterally terminate the contract. Furthermore, if the financial institution does not adequately provide the asset, thereby defaulting in its contractual obligation with the lessee, the lessee may also unilaterally terminate the contract.

Termination of the Ijara contract requires mutual consent of the parties involved. In such an instance, the lessee is not obligated to pay the continued terms of the contract and would only be liable for rent up to the date of termination. Furthermore, the lessee is responsible for any negligent misuse of the property, and any maintenance costs required.

In the event that the Ijara agreement is breached, this then requires dispute resolution and/or litigation. The process depends on the jurisdiction and the practices within that jurisdiction.

## Specifics Relating to Ijara as a Financing Vehicle

It is important to note that there are two distinct aspects to the Ijara contract. The first is the purchase between the bank and the developer, whereby in theory the bank is working as an agent of the lessee. The bank is liable as the owner of the asset, which means the bank should pay the closing costs, taxes, and any other payments typically borne by the owner. The obligations of the lessee do not take effect until after the transfer of the asset to the lessee and those would still be the obligations as a tenant and not an owner (e.g., maintenance fees). The second distinct aspect is the lease-to-purchase transaction between the bank and the lessee. This is the clear lessor/lessee relationship that is being entered into between the respective parties.

Upon termination of this type of an Ijara contract, the asset transfers to the lessee. The transfer in ownership may occur upon the last payment or for a nominal fee at the end of the contract or as a gift. The lease may have a clause to this effect. It is understood in this type of an Ijara agreement that title at the end of the term will transfer to the lessee upon completion of the terms. According to Shariah principles, a transaction may not be tied to a precondition on another transaction. However, Shariah scholars have allowed the parties to enter into a unilateral promise, whereby the lessor promises to sell the asset to the lessee at a future date for a predetermined amount. The lessee has the option to enter into or to reject the contract on the future date. The only party bound to the unilateral contract is the lessor.

So, to recap, a full lease-to-purchase agreement is the following: the bank purchases the property from the developer. Meanwhile, the bank enters into a lease agreement with the lessee and into a sale-undertaking agreement. The sale-undertaking agreement is the future unilateral promise to sell the property to the lessee.

## Types of Contracts Used in an Ijara Structure

There are various methods and contracts that may be used when preparing such a structure. Some contracts that are used together to form the necessary Ijara structure include a sale-purchase agreement, a sale undertaking by the financier, a purchase undertaking by the buyer, a lease (Ijara) agreement, and an agency service contract. It is important to note that the agency service contract is used to redistribute the liability of maintenance and service of the asset to the lessor and not the owner, as is typically required from an owner. Although this may seem like a minor point, it is imperative that such an agreement exists in the event that there are any maintenance issues relating to the asset. Otherwise, a Shariah court may hold that the owner is liable for all repairs and damages.

### Musharakah or a Mutanaqisa

The literal definition of Musharakah is a "sharing." The sharing consists of a profit-loss sharing arrangement among two or more parties. The sharing may be through financial investments, a division of labor, or a combination of both. The contract functions similar to that of a joint venture. Basically, two parties enter into an arrangement, whereby one party may elect to be silent or active, depending on the terms of the agreement. Both parties, regardless of their level of activity, will suffer a loss if the joint venture fails. However, if the joint venture is a success, then both parties will also receive a benefit from the success.

There are two main types of Musharakah, either by property or by contract. A Musharakah by property is called Shirakat al-Milk. This is simply an agreement between two partners to purchase property jointly. A Musharakah by contract is called Shirakah al-Akd. This type of Musharakah is subdivided into three types: Shirakat al-Amwal, Shirakat al-A'mal, and Shirakat Al-Akd. Shirakat al-Amwal is an agreement in which all partners invest capital into a commercial enterprise, similar to that of a joint venture agreement of a corporation. Shirakat al-A'mal is an agreement in which the partners undertake to render services and share the fees earned. The sharing of the fees is not correlated to the percentage of work contributed to the organization. Shirakat Al-Akd is the purchase and sale of a commodity at a deferred price. The sharing of the losses, however, is in proportion to each shareholder's investment.[190]

A Musharakah transaction can take several different forms, such as a continued Musharakah, Musharakah in working capital, and a diminishing Musharakah.[191] Each agreement requires the basic elements of a Musharakah listed below. They vary based on the level of commitment by the parties and their willingness to contribute time or capital to the project. We will briefly discuss the differences among the types of Musharakah and then the important overall elements required in a Musharakah arrangement, which includes partnership in capital, results of the project, and distribution.

The first transaction we will review is a continued hh. In this type of a Musharakah, the partners involved are committed to the project.[192] This type of a Musharakah does not have a termination date and is, in some instances, referred to as a permanent Musharakah.

An example of a continued Musharakah would be one in which three parties enter into an arrangement to open a manufacturing facility in Canada. The three partners will be entering the partnership at various investment ratios. The first partner, Joseph, will be the chief executive officer and is investing 33 percent of the capital. The second partner, Donna, is investing 27 percent of the capital and will be the chief financial officer. The third partner is only able to contribute 15 percent of the capital, but he will be the corporation's chief operations officer. The partners require additional capital and approach Islamic Bank to enter into the arrangement and provide additional financing of 25 percent as a silent partner. Islamic Bank will bear the potential gain of success as well as the potential loss of up to its 25 percent stake holding in the entity. Islamic Bank agrees to enter into the arrangement, provided the company provides audited annual financial statements. The shareholders will distribute the profits and losses in accordance with the percentage of capital placed by each individual, including Islamic Bank. There are various possible arrangements that may be undertaken by the parties and the above example is only one of the many possibilities available.

A second type of Musharakah arrangement is the Musharakah in working capital.[193] In this type of a Musharakah, the partnership is in reference to financing a subproject. For instance, using the above example, the manufacturing company is seeking to purchase a new machine to expand its business. The above capital and percentage structure is maintained. A new financier is approached to aid in financing the new product line, which requires different machinery and equipment. It is proposed that the new financier enters as a silent partner in the subproject, providing the financing, but not involved in the management of the operations. The subproject will be under a new corporation and the profits will be distributed upon success

The last type of a Musharakah is a diminishing Musharakah. This form allows the client to purchase back the position of the partner during the course of the partnership.[194] This form of Musharakah is most commonly used as a financing vehicle. For example, the bank lends a borrower money to purchase a home. The borrower pays installments to the bank and with each installment he purchases a percentage of ownership in the home.

## Necessary Elements in a Musharakah

As mentioned in each of the other structures, the Musharakah contract must bear in mind all the elements previously discussed such as Gharar, interest, honesty, and fair dealings, as well as incorporating the elements noted below.

## Distribution of Profit

It is important to remember two points: first, a Musharakah agreement is an agreement of sharing and second, a Shariah-compliant contract must contain all the elements of the contract. Therefore, as in any contract, a Musharakah contract must outline the full agreement between the parties. This includes the distribution of profit, any lump sums, the percentage of shares, and any potential losses. A Musharakah agreement is to contain potential losses as well as gains. There are no specifications to the manner or percentage in which the potential profits are to be divided. The distribution does not have to be related to the percentage of capital investment or the division of labor. The distribution is decided by the parties and established in accordance with their agreement.

Consideration should be given to a common view under Musharakah: if there is a silent partner who does not participate in the management of the project, the silent partner is limited to receiving his profit in relation to the portion of his investment. However, this is not an obligatory consensus. The parties have the right to distribute the profits at their individual discretion and the overall agreement of the parties in the contract will prevail.

Another significant point to consider in a Musharakah transaction is that the profit may not be designated as a particular lump sum. It must be allocated from an actual profit of the joint venture. In other words, at the end of the fiscal year (or the culmination of the project), the final profit will be allocated in accordance with the agreed upon percentage. Remember, under Shariah, any investor (regardless if he or she is a financier facilitating the transaction) must bear a burden of risk. An agreed upon lump sum does not fulfill that requirement and does not share a burden of the risk. Therefore, an agreed upon lump sum profit is unacceptable. It is possible to include a lump sum agreement, but such sum may be paid toward fees, final settlement, etc. In that event, the lump sum amount and details must be expressly mentioned in the contractual arrangement.

Profit examples include the following: Sylvia and Josephina enter into a new venture together. Sylvia wants to open an Italian restaurant near the marina. She is an excellent chef and has won many awards. Josephina agrees to help invest in the new restaurant. In the first scenario, Josephina elects to be a silent partner. She is confident in Sylvia's cooking skills, but is unsure of her management skills, so Josephina wants to protect her investment. Josephina wants to ensure that she regains a 33 percent profit at the end of the first year, regardless of actual profits.

Both Josephina and Sylvia have come to an attorney to prepare their Musharakah agreement.[10] Immediately, the attorney informs both parties that under a Musharakah arrangement, a determined lump sum profit is unacceptable. However, if Josephina incurs various costs in relation to the agreement, she may be provided with a lump sum payment or she may also take a security over certain assets and, using both a Musharakah and an Ijara structure, achieve her objective. The parties decide not to complicate

---

10.   Some may find this scenario unethical. However, this is a realistic situation that is encountered in the daily practice. This is not an issue of morality; rather, it is an example of finding a compromise in order to fulfill the objectives of the parties as well as satisfy the Shariah compliance requirements.

the structure at this point in time. However, Josephina determines that there are certain costs that she is incurring by entering into this Musharakah and, as a result, is due a lump sum fee in addition to a share of the profits. Therefore, the final arrangement structure includes Sylvia as the active partner and Josephina as a silent partner with a lump sum payment in the first year to cover fees and costs. Thereafter, Josephina will receive a percentage of the profits in accordance with her invested share in the Musharakah. Sylvia will receive the remaining profits as she is an investor and an active participant in the Musharakah.

In the second scenario, the same facts as above apply, except Josephina elects to be an active participant in the business. She has a sound business mind and has several successful ventures due to her business acumen. In this instance, the profit may be divided as per the percentage of capital investment, as per participation, or as per agreement.

What if, at the end of the first year, there is no profit to be distributed to the parties? If there is no profit to be distributed, then there is no distribution to the partners. By definition, a profit is what remains after all expenses; therefore, an amount of zero may not be distributed. However, if a lump sum debt is contracted, then that is to be paid at the agreed upon time regardless of profit, as that is a debt on the Musharakah and not considered to be an equity payment. Relating this concept to the above scenarios, Josephina will be entitled to her lump sum payment regardless of the Musharakah not earning a profit this year. The lump sum is tied to costs and fees that are reasonable and that she encountered. The profit in the subsequent years will be allocated in accordance to the percentage as designated by the Musharakeen ("partners"). This agreement should be included in a separate shareholder's agreement outlining all the terms and conditions of the parties.

The most important aspect of the Musharakah is that all partners (regardless of their activity in the Musharakah) are subject to profit and loss. However, unlike other conventional agreements, the loss in a Musharakah is limited by each partner's respective investment.[195] No partner may lose greater than his or her investment. This concept is an Islamic concept that preserves the level of risk undertaken. It is important to understand that this is rooted in fostering the growth of the marketplace by encouraging participants to enter into agreements and to take risks that are determinable and that will not result in a debt in the event the Musharakah fails. This is an important Islamic economic principle that preserves the marketplace and seeks to sustain a healthy economy.

# What Type of Capital is Accepted in a Musharakah?

The type of capital allowed as part of a Musharakah is a disputed point among scholars. May the capital be provided in property, cash, product, inventory, etc.? There are several underlying concerns. First, how is the fair market value determined during the course of the partnership? In the event that the fair market value of the commodity increases or decreases does that change affect the percentage share of the partner who provided the commodity?

Using the previous example with Sylvia and Josephina, let's assume Josephina's capital investment of USD$100,000, but Sylvia was tight on cash because she had purchased brand new equipment for the restaurant's kitchen at a cost of USD$100,000. However, while the equipment is all new today, in five or ten years, it will not demand the same market value. Rather, it will significantly depreciate. So what should be the amount of capital investment registered on the books from Sylvia? This is actually per agreement between the parties. The parties may agree that the current market value will be considered as the capital investment on behalf of Sylvia, because this is the current amount that she is contributing to the Musharakah. However, they may also agree to depreciate the value slightly as the equipment will be less than market value after opening night.

What if the partner wants to be bought out of the Musharakah? What interval of time is used to determine the market value of the commodity and the percentage of ownership? Again, using the previous example, if Sylvia later decides to leave the partnership or even if she wants to purchase Josephina's shares, the fluctuation in her capital investment will affect the overall percentage of shareholding. Therefore, it is extremely important that these questions are addressed at the beginning of any transaction that allows a nonliquid capital investment.

Another important aspect to consider is if the nonliquid capital investment is provided as a rare commodity. How is the value determined? With a rare commodity, there is no marketplace to determine the actual value of the commodity and therefore it is not possible to determine the proper capital contribution. An example of a rare commodity would be Leonardo da Vinci's painting of the Mona Lisa used as a capital contribution. We all know the Mona Lisa is expensive and rare. While we also may estimate the value of the Mona Lisa, there is no real market. Therefore, it would be difficult to ascertain the value accurately and determine the actual capital contribution. The moderate solution to this question is identifying if the commodity may be replaced in like and kind. This balance of like and kind aids in the liquidity of the commodity. An example of a like and kind commodity is grain, which has a consistent market and a fairly consistent value. It may be replaced or traded equally. Grain is an example of a perfect illiquid commodity that may be provided in the alternative as capital investment.

## Management of the Musharakah

As discussed previously, the management of the Musharakah is dependent on the agreement of the partners and their willingness to participate in the Musharakah. The partners have the right to participate unless it is agreed upon otherwise. It is important to remember that the only restriction is regarding the silent partner's profit. The profit allocated to a silent partner may not be greater than his or her capital contribution to the venture. The reason behind this is that the partner is not adding any further value to the partnership other than the capital investment. However, if a partner decides to take an active role in the business, then he or she may take a greater profit than his or her share of the capital investment.

Another important aspect relating to the management of a Musharakah is that the active partner is considered to be an agent of all partners in all business-related matters. This includes being an agent for all silent partners as well. The active partner is considered in the marketplace to be authorized by all the business partners to engage in all aspects of the business activities. So any agreement signed by one partner is accepted as an agreement of all partners to be bound by this agreement. This includes silent partners as well. This follows the same western concepts of agency. Therefore, the silent partners will also be liable to the extent of their share of all contractual liabilities entered into on their behalf.

From a management perspective, the partners, whether active or silent, need to work to ensure that the management of the Musharakah will be a success. Even if the partner is a financier, the joining in the partnership is not passive. Rather, there is a responsibility on the partner to ensure that the project is feasible and to aid in ensuring its success. Therefore, a silent partner is not necessarily a passive partner.

Lastly, the partners in the Musharakah may agree to appoint a manager to run the business venture—someone who is specialized in the field—and delegate all or some authority to this manager. This is also acceptable under the terms of a Musharakah. The most important point to consider is that the partners are diligent in ensuring the success of the arrangement and work toward such success.

# Termination of the Musharakah

Every beginning has an ending and in a Musharakah every partner has the right to terminate the agreement so long as notice is provided to all parties. As in any standard conventional contract, notice should be clearly defined and stated in the contract. Remember, it is important to attempt to prevent a Gharar in any transaction, including a Musharakah.

How does a termination of the Musharakah take place? There are several different methods. Ideally, the contractual arrangement between the parties would include details on how best to terminate the Musharakah. This may include the partners retaining the first right of refusal to purchase the outstanding shares of the terminating partner. Another possibility may include agreeing on a termination price or allowing the shares to be purchased directly in the marketplace. This is an important consideration at the initial contracting stage, especially if one of the partners provides an illiquid capital contribution or an illiquid asset is involved. Furthermore, most partnerships include both liquid and illiquid assets, so the question arises as to how such assets may be allocated on a pro rata basis. In that instance, if the parties have not previously considered the division of assets or the possibility of the termination of the Musharakah, Shariah will seek what is in the best interest of the joint venture and balance it against dividing the assets in a manner that sustains the Musharakah long-term.

For example, using the above scenario, the assets of the partnership with Sylvia and Josephina include the liquid capital of USD$100,000 and the USD$100,000 oven. The partners used the liquid capital to purchase additional equipment, as working capital, and to build out the restaurant. Sylvia seeks to terminate the Musharakah. The contract between the parties indicates that either party may terminate the agreement and sell her shares to the opposite party. The nonterminating party has the first right of refusal to the shares. In this instance, Josephina has the first right of refusal.

Josephina is interested in purchasing Sylvia's shares. She wants to change the direction of the restaurant to a bakery. The restaurant has liquid and illiquid assets to which Sylvia is entitled. Furthermore, the contractual arrangement between the parties was decided to be a 50/50 split. The parties are not obligated to sell all the illiquid assets to determine Sylvia's buyout. Rather, the Shariah seeks to maintain the viability of the restaurant and find a liquid means to apportion the property so as not to disturb the longevity of the business. In the event both parties are seeking to terminate the relationship completely, as the assets are all sold and liquefied, each party will take her apportioned percentage. In this case, the split is equal.

Preferably, it is up to the partners to identify the manner in which to terminate the Musharakah and it is best if such an issue is dealt with at the beginning of the relationship whether through the memorandum of association or a shareholder's agreement. Further, it is important to ensure that there are no restrictions on such agreements within the practicing jurisdiction. The termination of the agreement should also include any provisions relating to an early termination.

What if all the partners are seeking to completely dissolve the partnership? Again, it is best to outline such terms in the initial agreements signed by the partners. This also lies under the concept of freedom to contract under a Shariah perspective. There are specific points to consider in relation to the assets in a dissolution of the relationship. If the assets are liquid, termination is simple, as the assets will be distributed in accordance with the pro rata share of each partner. However, if the assets are illiquid, the parties should agree on the distribution. Ideally, the parties would have considered this possibility in the initial agreements. However, life does not always work seamlessly, so if a disagreement arises, the preferred method is to distribute the illiquid assets in a manner that is proportionate to the pro rata share of each party.

## A Musharakah Agreement as a Financing Arrangement

A Musharakah agreement may also present itself in a financing and not exclusively as a joint venture. The most typical is a diminishing Musharakah, which is common in home financing arrangements. In this type of a financing arrangement, the financier will purchase the asset with a deposit from the customer. The monthly payments made by the customer will include a fair market value of the rental of the property as well as a portion allocated as a buyback of each monthly payment or upon the completion of the payment of a unit.[196] A unit may be defined in any form to facilitate enforceability, which is further clarified below.

For example, Gizelle would like to purchase a home using Musharakah financing with Hilda's Finance. The home has the requisite value and Gizelle qualifies as a sound partner in the Musharakah-financed agreement. Gizelle requires USD$100,000 to purchase the home. Gizelle has a 20 percent down payment, but needs to finance the remaining 80 percent. So she approaches Hilda's Finance, which is willing to provide the necessary 80 percent. Gizelle now owns 20 percent of the home and Hilda's Finance owns the remaining 80 percent. The parties will also determine the monthly rental payments and the financing conditions. The financing conditions include the term of the financing arrangement and the amount necessary to pay down the 80 percent to increase ownership in the home monthly. As each month passes, the rental payment decreases as Gizelle's ownership rights increase. Therefore, if the rental of the home was USD$1,000 and she owned 20 percent, then in the first month her rental payment to Hilda is USD$800. The remaining USD$200 is her portion as owner. Furthermore, each month the rental payment amount to Hilda's Finance will decrease in proportion to the percentage purchased monthly by Gizelle.

Although this is a common financing method, the enforceability of such a mechanism is difficult. As the ownership of the borrower increases and the ownership of the financier decreases, then the lien on the asset must be reperfected to reflect the ownership change. The cost of monthly perfecting the security would be too much for either the financier or the borrower to bear. In this example, Gizelle would be purchasing her ownership monthly in the home and decreasing the ownership of Hilda's Finance. Hilda's Finance currently has a lien on the home for its ownership percentage. In accordance with this structure, in order to ensure enforcement in the event of default, Hilda's Finance would need to monthly resecure its percentage of ownership remaining in the property. The cost of monthly perfection would be borne by the owners (Gizelle and Hilda) at the ownership percentage at that time. On a 15-year term, this would entail 180 perfections in order for this structure to be enforceable throughout the term..

The reality is that financing institutions do not readjust the lien. Depending on the jurisdiction, enforcement in the event of default differs. Some jurisdictions would declare that such a structure is conventional and does not abide by the Musharakah Munaqasa (diminishing Musharakah) principles. However, the parties may agree that the diminishing Musharakah will occur in units and, upon the completion of payment of each unit, the parties may then resecure the remaining units as a lien against the asset. This reduces the cost of continuous perfection as well as works to maintain the compliance of the documents and assist in assurances for enforceability if such a need arises.

## Mudarabah

A Mudarabah is another type of asset-based financing contract used in Islamic finance.[197] This type of an agreement is a principal-agent relationship.[198] The method of investment by the partner is what distinguishes a Mudarabah from a Musharakah contract. Often, this type of a contract is the means for a small business to receive a capital injection for a project, which aids the business owner in growth and development.[199]

A partner in a Mudarabah provides capital investment for the commercial enterprise, but does not partake in the management of the actual enterprise.[200] In essence, this is a silent partner arrangement. A Mudarabah involves a partner described as Rabb al Mal (owner of the capital) and a manager described as a Mudarib.[201] The partner in this instance is a silent partner and only provides the investment to be used and managed by the manager or managers.[202]

For example, Jamal requires additional capital for his business. He has a new contract with a large client, but does not have enough capital to prepare the first order. Jamal approaches Mudarabah Finance Center. Mudarabah offers to inject capital into the business after careful review of the five-year business plan, the client list, and the new client's payment terms. After seeing the potential growth for the business, Mudarabah Finance Center wants to provide capital, but not participate in any of the management of the business. Rather, Mudarabah Finance Center will be exclusively a silent partner benefiting from the profits of the business. Mudarabah Finance Center is depending on Jamal's management capabilities and his experience in the business. In the event of any losses, Mudarabah Finance Center will suffer no greater loss than its capital injection into the business.

It is important to remember that the underlying business affairs of the company must be Shariah-compliant. In other words, the business must be a permissible type of business not dealing with such things as alcohol, drugs, etc. Furthermore, there is nothing that limits a partner from entering into a Mudarabaha arrangement where there are multiple managers participating in the same agreement. In that instance, any profits distributed are based on the agreed upon proportion between the parties.[203] The partner will only be responsible for losses up to the amount of his or her investment, just like all the other Shariah-compliant transactions.[204]

In another example of a Mudarabah contract, a small business manufacturer receives a large order to manufacture goods. The small business owner does not have the requisite capital to purchase the materials necessary to complete the project. He requests from the lender a Mudarabah agreement to borrow funds to complete the project. The small business owner will manage the production of the goods and the fulfillment of the order. In return, the lender evaluates the risk of the transaction and then decides whether to lend the necessary funds. The lender becomes a silent partner in the transaction, profiting upon completion.

# Necessary Elements in Mudarabah

A mudarabah is an interesting structure as it is a structure for a shorter period of time and may be in relation to many different types of assets. It is again important to remember all the elements previously described as part of the Mudarabah contract, including the detailed structural elements discussed below.

## *Asset*

A Mudarabah as an asset-based financing scheme requires an asset or collateral as part of the contract.[205] Although it is not compulsory, it is highly common to ensure protection of the capital investment by the partners.[206] An asset or collateral is often requested by lenders in a Mudarabah contract. It is important to note that if a security over an asset is taken, it must be properly perfected in accordance with the laws of the jurisdiction. Additionally, the elements of an existing and present asset are required under this financing scheme.

# Distribution of Profits

The most important aspect in a Mudarabah and in all Islamic contracts is outlining all the terms and conditions of the contract at the outset.[207] The contractual arrangements are binding on the parties, so it is important to determine all the elements of the contract to avoid Gharar as much as possible. Therefore, the distribution of profit is an important element that also must be clearly identified within the contract.

There are important elements of a Mudarabah that need to be considered when reviewing the distribution of profit. The first is that the manager does not earn a salary or an income. His participation and management of the Mudarabah are his contribution toward the arrangement in contrast to the investor's capital injection. Therefore, the manager's efforts, time, and expenses should be considered when contemplating the division of profits.

In some instances, the manager may receive a higher percentage of profits depending on the nature of the transaction. Furthermore, providing the manager with the greater percentage of profits is a way to incentivize the manager and seek to ensure the success of the project.[208] The division of profits may be used as an incentive to drive various business sectors of the arrangement. For instance, an investor and a manager enter into a Mudarabah in relation to selling various brands of automobiles that range in value from Hondas to Bentleys. The profit margin made on the Honda is much less than that made on the Bentley Since the profit margin on the Honda is lower, the investor is worried that the manager will focus all the sales on the Bentley and not work to sell the Honda which has a larger market base. Therefore, the investor decides to incentivize the manager to sell more Hondas. So the investor and the manager agree to vary the distribution of the profits in accordance with the brand of the vehicle.

It must also be noted that the distribution of profits is contingent on balancing the profits and losses among all projects prior to the distribution. The Mudarabah may consist of one or more projects; however, the details must be outlined in the contract. If the Mudarabah consists of one or more projects, then all the profits and losses among the projects must be determined and weighed prior to the distribution of the profits.

## Management of a Mudarabah

The manager in a Mudarabah does not make any capital investment in the project. Rather, the manager brings value through his or her capabilities, management skills, and technical know how. Therefore, the manager is not to receive any salary or regular payments for managing the enterprise, as this is considered to be his value contribution to the arrangement.[209] This is a unanimous point under all schools of Islamic Fiqh. This does not mean that the manager may not have a right to purchase equity in the joint venture. If the parties agree, the manager may have the right to purchase a portion or the entire joint venture from the other partner (further details are provided under the termination of a Mudarabah).[210]

However, there are conflicting views in allowing the manager to receive payment for expenses incurred. Some schools of thought recognize that the manager has not provided any capital investment and that expenses incurred are part of his contribution to the venture. However, others believe that such expenses should only be paid when the manager is traveling, but not within the manager's resident city.

It is important in a Mudarabah contract that the manager partake in the success of the venture. So the contract with the manager may include positive incentives for the manager to actively engage in ensuring a positive result for the venture.[211] This may include additional compensation; however, it may not include a consistent salary for his expertise.

The role of the manager is very important. The manager's ability to run the operations of the venture is critical to the success or failure of the project. But the manager also carries a responsibility to the investor, even though he has not provided any capital for the project.[212] Therefore, it should be noted that any negligence or mismanagement of the joint venture by the manager will be deemed to be the sole responsibility of the manager of the Mudarabah.[213] The manager in that instance will be solely responsible to the partners.[214]

## Restricted or Unrestricted Mudarabah Contract

A Mudarabah contract can be either restricted or unrestricted. In a restricted Mudarabah contract, the financing institution may impose restrictions on the terms and conditions of the arrangement. If such conditions are imposed and the customer breaches any of the covenants, then the customer is in breach of the arrangement. The restrictions on the arrangement may include restrictions on the use of the capital and the manner and purposes for which it is to be used. Furthermore, in the event that the customer does not abide by these restrictions and a loss occurs, then the customer is responsible for the loss. A restricted type of arrangement is more prevalent when the project is specified and narrow in scope. Such an arrangement aids the financier in ensuring that the funds will be utilized for the requisite purpose.

As you may have guessed, an unrestricted Mudarabah is the opposite— the financing institution does not impose certain restrictions or limitations on the borrower. In this instance, in the event of loss, the financier does not have recourse against the borrower, except in instances of fraud and mismanagement. This is a more general type of Mudarabah arrangement used for purposes such as aiding in the financing of working capital.

## Termination of a Mudarabah Contract

Typically, a Mudarabah contract is not binding upon the parties; it is more of an at-will contractual arrangement.[215] Therefore, several aspects should be considered in relation to termination of the contract. The most basic element is that the length of a Mudarabah contract is usually determined by mutual consent. So long as the parties consent to continue the arrangement, the agreement is in existence. If the parties seek to dissolve the agreement, the mutual consent is broken and the agreement is terminated.

This may be an issue of concern, because in the operation of any business it takes time for the project or business venture to materialize and begin to be profitable. Therefore, either the investor or the manager may want to restrict the termination of the arrangement in order to properly ensure the project's success. In this instance, if a party during this period terminates the relationship, it may risk the entire success of the project.

Also, if the investor seeks to terminate the project and removes his funds, the venture may not only fail, but the efforts of the manager are in vain. The manager would lose the viability of the project and also, as previously noted, would not have received compensation for his efforts. Therefore, the parties may want to limit or restrict the right of termination for a period of time to ensure the success of the venture. Such a contractual arrangement under Shariah law is acceptable.

For instance, Holly is looking to invest in a new project. She wants to build a new flower shop, but she does not know how to arrange flowers and has no experience in managing a store. Holly has a really good friend, Fern, who has been working at a flower shop in a large store for years managing the department. She dreams of one day working in a small shop on her own. Both Holly and Fern decide to enter into a Mudarabah arrangement, whereby Fern will manage the store and Holly will provide the capital. After much research, Fern realizes that it will take 1.5 years for the shop to begin to earn a profit and be successful. She discusses this with Holly and they both agree that it is important during this crucial time period that both parties participate in ensuring the success of the arrangement. They agree to place a provision in the contract that restricts the ability of either party to leave the arrangement. It is important to note that such a clause must be clearly specified in the Mudarabah agreement. The clause must be clearly articulated and agreed upon by the parties. This provision does not violate any rules of Shariah and will be binding on the parties.

Furthermore, in the event a party seeks to terminate the contract, he or she may do so by providing notice to all the parties involved in the contract. In the event that one party seeks to terminate the contract, this does not preclude the remaining parties from continuing the venture. Again, upon termination of the agreement, the parties must consider whether the assets are illiquid or liquid. Usually, the Mudarabah does not provide for a division of profits until the arrangement has concluded. However, if a party is seeking early termination of the contract, then a discussion will be required regarding the outstanding profits.

If the agreement allows for the manager to purchase the venture from the investor, appropriate provisions relating to the termination of a Mudarabah in this instance will be required in the contractual arrangement. Can an investor charge a fee in the event of such a termination? The answer is yes, an investor may charge a reasonable fee and it would not be considered to be a type of Riba (earning money on money).[216]

The distribution of assets is an important element in a Mudarabah contract. If the assets are liquid and the profits are earned on the principal, then the distribution is easily identified per the ratio specified in the contract. Issues begin to arise as the assets become less liquid. If the assets are illiquid and the contract is terminated, the manager may liquidate the assets and each party receives the pro rata share of the profits as outlined in the contract. These issues were previously addressed in the Musharakah and the division of liquid and illiquid assets. They are treated the same under this agreement.

# Part IV: Conclusion

# Conclusion

## *Islamic Finance Markets*

Islamic finance was the fastest growing industry over the past decade with an average of 14 percent growth annually.[217] Currently, over 1,100 institutions globally provide Islamic financial structures to the marketplace.[218] As of 2009, it is reported that about USD$882 billion comprised the Islamic financial markets and approximately USD$1 out of every trillion was utilized in a Shariah-compliant asset structure.[219]

Islamic finance is a long-term industry with great potential. The target market is not only the ever-increasing Muslim population, but individuals who are seeking more prudent investment choices that are linked to asset-based transactions. Also, with the current global distrust in the conventional system, many are seeking alternatives. Islamic finance is a strong and viable alternative in the marketplace and should not be underestimated.

The Islamic finance industry in the United States continues to be a niche market. Despite its international growth and potential opportunities, the U.S. Islamic finance market is populated with a limited group of professionals who have the requisite experience in this field. So if you have begun your quest in the understanding of Islamic finance, know that you are in the forefront of the marketplace with many growth opportunities internationally.

In this book, I highlighted the basics of Islamic finance to provide the background necessary in understanding how to later manipulate and build more complex structures. As I am sure you noted, the basic elements of many of the transactions are similar, such as asset requirements existing at the time of contract, attempting to eliminate Gharar from a contract, etc. The topics addressed in this book are the most common structures found in Islamic finance. However, there are more structures in Islamic finance, such as Bai Salam, Wakala, and Istisn'a, which will be covered in a later edition.

# Appendix A: Murabaha Chart

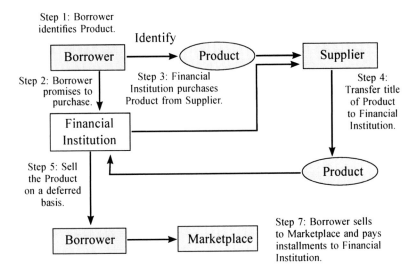

Step 1: Borrower identifies Product.

Identify

Borrower

Product

Supplier

Step 2: Borrower promises to purchase.

Step 3: Financial Institution purchases Product from Supplier.

Step 4: Transfer title of Product to Financial Institution.

Financial Institution

Step 5: Sell the Product on a deferred basis.

Product

Borrower

Marketplace

Step 7: Borrower sells to Marketplace and pays installments to Financial Institution.

# Appendix B: Ijara Chart
**Simple Ijara used to finance the purchase of an asset.**

Step 1: Sale and Purchase Agreement.

Developer sells Asset to Financial Institution and transfers title for purchase price.

Sale and Purchase Agreement.

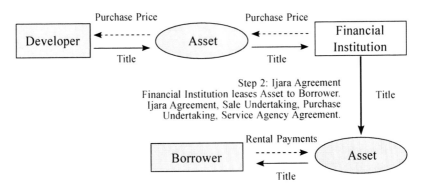

Step 2: Ijara Agreement
Financial Institution leases Asset to Borrower.
Ijara Agreement, Sale Undertaking, Purchase
Undertaking, Service Agency Agreement.

Step 3: Sale & Purchase Agreement.
Financial Institution transfers title of Asset to Borrower.
at culmination of the Ijara Agreement.
Sale and Purchase Agreement.

# Appendix C: Tawarruq Chart

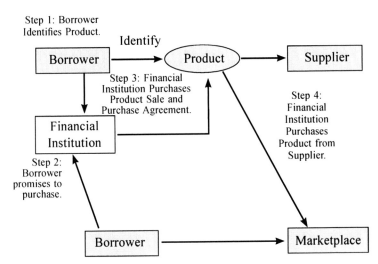

Step 1: Borrower Identifies Product.

Identify

Borrower

Step 3: Financial Institution Purchases Product Sale and Purchase Agreement.

Product

Supplier

Step 4: Financial Institution Purchases Product from Supplier.

Financial Institution

Step 2: Borrower promises to purchase.

Borrower

Marketplace

Step 5: Transfer Title of Products to Financial Institution, to Borrower, to Marketplace. Borrower pays installments to Financial Institution.

# Appendix D: Musharakah

**Musharakah Financing Structures: Scenario #1**

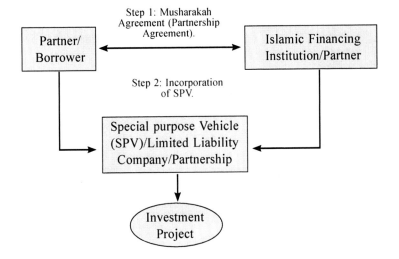

**Musharakah Financing Structures: Scenario #2**

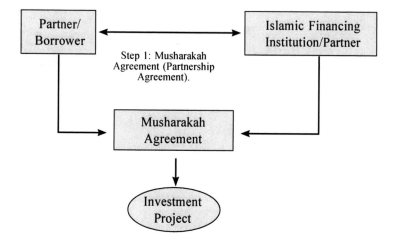

**Musharakah Mutanaqisa Financing Structure.**

Step 4: Transfer of ownership at completion
of Musharakah payments.

Step 3: Lease
Agreement and Rental
Payments.

| Partner/ Borrower | Islamic Financing Institution |

Step 1: Musharakah
Agreement (Partnership
Agreement).

Step 2:
Capital Share.

Step 2: Capital
Share.

**Musharakah Agreement**

Asset

# Appendix E: Mudharabah

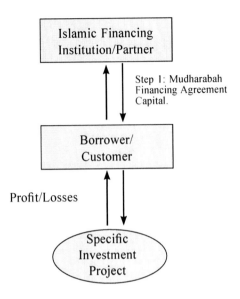

# Glossary of Terms

**Fatwa(s):** jurisprudence rulings by qualified Muslim scholars.

**Gharar:** uncertainty or deception.

**Ijara:** a lease-to-purchase financing method.

**Ijama:** consensus on a point of law by those authorized to interpret the Quran and Sunnah.

**Istisna:** longer-term financing where the price is agreed upon before the asset is actually built.

**Mathahab:** rights

**Mumayiz:** a party that is of legal age and with the requisite legal capacity to understand the implications of his or her actions.

**Murabaha:** buy/sell-back arrangement.

**Musharakah Mutanaqisa:** lease-to purchase or a diminishing-partnership arrangement.

**Qiyas:** a method used to determine whether a matter is compliant with Shariah. This method uses a strict reasoning by analogy.

**Quran:** the Holy Scripture for Muslims.

**Sunna:** the accepted tradition of the Prophet Muhammad[11] which details the Prophet's sayings and actions.

**Riba:** usury or interest.

**Takaful:** the Islamic method of taking insurance over an asset.

**Taqlid:** submissive acceptance of an earlier interpretation of Shariah law.

**Tawarruq:** a three-party contract, where the asset that is leveraged may be sold and the remaining assets become an unsecured debt or paid.

---

11.  Peace be Upon Him.

# Endnotes

1.  Kabir Hassan & Mervyn Lewis, Handbook of Islamic Banking, 1 (Edward Elgar Publishing Limited, 2007).

2.  *Id.*

3.  http://www.imf.org/external/pubs/ft/fandd/2005/12/qorchi.htm

4.  http://www.cgap.org/p/site/c/template.rc/1.26.3303/

5.  Amir H. Khoury, "Ancient and Islamic Source of Intellectual Property Protection in the Middle East: A Focus on Trademarks," 43 IDEA: The Journal of Law and Technology 151, 2003 at 4.

6.  Teachings of the Prophet Muhammad (PBUH) are usually referenced as Sunnah.

7.  Khoury, *supra* note 5, at 4.

8.  *Id.* at 5.

9.  *Id.*

10. Raslan, Heba, "Shari'a and the Protection of Intellectual Property: The Example of Egypt," 47 IDEA: The Intellectual Property Law Review 497, 2007, 513

11. Khoury, *supra* note 5, at 5.

12. *Id.*

13. *Id.*

14. Raslan, *supra* note 10, at 505.

15. Khoury, *supra* note 5, at 5.

16. Raslan, *supra* note 10, at 505.

17. Khoury, *supra* note 5, at 5.

18. Raslan, *supra* note 10, at 505.

19. *Id.*

20. *Id.*

21. *Id.*

22. *Id.*

23. *Id.*

24. *Id.*

25. *Id.*

26. *Id.* at 506.

27. *Id.*

28. *Id.*

29. Richard E. Vaughan, "Defining Terms in the Intellectual Property Protection Debate: Are the North and South Arguing Past Each Other When We Say 'Property?' A Lockean, Confucian, and Islamic Comparison," 2 ILSA Journal of International & Comparative Law, 1996 at 350.

30. *Id.*

31. Raslan, *supra* note 10, at 506.

32. *Id.*

33. Khoury, *supra* note 5, at 5.

34. Raslan, *supra* note 10, at 506.

35. Khoury, *supra* note 5, at 5.

36. *Id.*

37. Vaughan, *supra* note 29, at 350.

38. Raslan, *supra* note 10, at 508; *See also*, Vaughan, *supra* note 29 at 350.

39. George F. Hourani, The Basis of Authority of Consensus in Sunnite Islam, 13 (Studia Islamica, No. 21, 1964); See also Raslan, *supra* note 10, at 506.

40. Raslan, *supra* note 10. at 508.

41. *Id.*

42. *Id.*

43. *Id.*

44. Khoury, *supra* note 5, at 5.

45. *Id.*

46. *Id.*

47. Raslan, *supra* note 10, at 509. See also, M. Cherif Bassiouni & Gamal M. Badr, "The Shariahh: Sources, Interpretation, and Rule-Making," 1 UCLA J. Islamic & NEAR E.L. 135, 148 (2002).

48. *Id.*

49. Raslan, *supra* note 10, at 509.

50. *Id.* at 510.

51. *Id.*

52. Khoury, *supra* note 5, at 5.

53. *Id.* at 6.

54. *Id.*

55. *Id.*

56. *Id.* at 19.

57. *Id.*

58. *Id.*

59. *Id.*

60. *Id.*

61. *Id.*

62. *Id.*

63. Raslan, *supra* note 10, at 510

64. *Id.*

65. *Id.* at 511.

66. *Id.*

67. *Id.*

68. *Id.*

69. *Id.*

70. *Id.*

71. Khoury, *supra* note 5, at 6.

72. *Id.*

73. *Id.*

74. *Id.*

75. Angelo M. Venardos, Current Issues in Islamic Banking and Finance: Resilience and Stability in the Present System, World Scientific Publishing Company Pte. Ltd., 2010, page 78.

76. Mohammed El Qorchi, "Islamic Finance Gears Up," December 2005, Finance & Development (Quarterly magazine of the IMF), Volume 42, Number 4.; http://www.imf.org/external/pubs/ft/fandd/2005/12/qorchi.htm

77. Khoury, *supra* note 5, at 11.

78. *Id.*

79. Natalie Schoon, Islamic Banking and Finance, 26 (Spiramus Press Ltd., Jan. 2009).

80. Raslan, *supra* note 10, at 523.

81. Arthur J. Gemmell, "Commercial Arbitration in the Islamic Middle East," 5 Santa Clara J. Int'l L. 1, 20 (2006). See also, http://www.scu.edu/scjil/archive/Gemmell.pdf

82. Angelo M. Venardos, Islamic Banking & Finance in South-East Asia: Its Development and Future, 53 (World Scientific Publishing Co. Pte. Ltd., ed.2, 2005)

83. *Id.* See also Schoon, *supra* note 79, at 17.

84. Venardos, Islamic Banking, *supra* note 82 at 53

85. *Id.*

86. *Id.*

87. *Id.*

88. *Id.*

89. Raslan, *supra* note 10, at 523

90. Venardos, Current Issues, *supra* note 75, at 118.

91. Schoon, *supra* note 79, at 22.

92. Nael G Bunni, The FIDIC Form of Contract: the Fourth Edition of the Red Book, 46 (Blackwell Science, 1992).

93. *Id.*

94. *Id.*

95. Schoon, *supra* note 79, at 22.

96. Bunni, *supra* note 92, at 46.

97. *Id.*

98. *Id.*

99. Venardos, Islamic Banking, *supra* note 82, at 57.

100. Hassan & Lewis, *supra* note 1, at 248.

101. *Id.*

102. Bunni, *supra* note 92, at 46.

103. Schoon, *supra* note 79, at 26

104. Understanding Islamic Finance, Muhammed Ayub page 2. AU: Please provide full citation.

105. Khoury, *supra* note 5, at 11.

106. *Id.*

107. *Id.*

108. Raslan, *supra* note 10, at 524.

109. *Id.*

110. *Id.*

111. *Id.* This will be later discussed in the next section dealing with Hisbah.

112. Khoury, *supra* note 5, at 11.

113. *Id.*

114. *Id.*

115. *Id.*

116. *Id.*

117. *Id.*

118. *Id.*

119. Venardos, Current Issues, *supra* note 75, at 155.

120. Hassan & Lewis, *supra* note 1, at 43.

121. *Id.*

122. *Id.*

123. *Id.*

124. *Id.*

125. *Id.*

126. *Id.*

127. *Id.*

128. Venardos, Islamic Banking, *supra* note 82, at 59. *See also* Hassan & Lewis, *supra* note 1, at 50.

129. Schoon, *supra* note 79, at 20

130. Hassan & Lewis, *supra* note 1, at 43

131. *Id.*

132. *Id.*

133. *Id.*

134. *Id.*

135. *Id.*

136. Hassan & Lewis, *supra* note 1, at 44-45. Sheikh al Tantawi from the Al Azhar mosque in Cairo has argued that bank interest is a form of profit-sharing and characterized as a commercial profit. Therefore, since it is profit-sharing, it is permissible. This view is almost unanimously rejected by other scholars.

137. Hassan & Lewis, *supra* note 1, at 46.

138. *Id.*

139. *Id.*

140. Ramadan, Hisham, Understanding Islamic law: from Classical to Contemporary page 97. AU: Please provide complete citation. This interpretation may be found in the Quranic translation and commentary by Yusuf Ali.

141. Hassan & Lewis, *supra* note 1, at 50-51.

142. Venardos, Islamic Banking, *supra* note 82, at 59. *See also* Hassan & Lewis, *supra* note 1, at 50.

143. Venardos, Current Issues, *supra* note 75, at 282.

144. *Id.*

145. Gemmell, *supra* note 81, at 8. *See also* http://www.scu.edu/scjil/archive/Gemmell.pdf

146. Khoury, *supra* note 5, at 9.

147. *Id.* at 20.

148. *Id.*

149. Gemmell, *supra* note 81, at 8. *See also* http://www.scu.edu/scjil/archive/Gemmell.pdf

150. World Bank, http://go.worldbank.org/D6OE3H4VQ0

151. Venardos, Current Issues, *supra* note 75, at 119.

152. *Id.* at 176.

153. Hakimah Yaacob and Edib Smolo, Opalesque, May 31, 2010 AU: Please provide complete citation. http://www.opalesque.com/OIFI164/Lex_Islamicus_It_is_not_a_murabaha145.html.

154. Hans Visser & Herschel Visser, Islamic Finance: Principles and Practice, 58 (Edward Elgar Publishing Ltd., 2009).

155. Ahmed Al-Suwaidi, Finance of International Trade in the Gulf, 93 (Graham & Trotman Ltd. 1994).

156. *Id.*

157. *Id.*

158. Hassan & Lewis, *supra* note 1, at 52.

159. Venardos, Current Issues, *supra* note 75, at 115.

160. Visser & Visser, *supra* note 155, at 58.

161. *Id.*

162. *Id.*

163. *Id.*

164. Venardos, Current Issues, *supra* note 75, at 176.

165. Visser & Visser, *supra* note 155, at 58.

166. Hassan & Lewis, *supra* note 1, at 52.

167. Al-Suwaidi, *supra* note 156, at 93.

168. Visser & Visser, *supra* note 155, at 58.

169. Venardos, Islamic Banking, *supra* note 82, at 59.

170. Brian Kettell, Islamic Finance in a Nutshell: A Guide for Non-Specialists, 230 (John Wiley & Sons Ltd., 2010).

171. Mahmoud A. El-Gamal, Islamic Finance: Law, Economics, and Practice, 34 (Cambridge University Press, 2006).

172. Kettell, Nutshell, *supra* note 171, at 230.

173. *Id.*

174. Schoon, *supra* note 79, at 107.

175. *Id.*

176. *Id.*

177. El-Gamal, *supra* note 172, at 34.

178. *Id.*

179. Kettell, Nutshell, *supra* note 171, at 209.

180. *Id.*

181. Venardos, Current Issues, *supra* note 75, at 175.

182. In the event that the parties have entered into a lease-to-purchase agreement, the payments are still considered rental payments.

183. Visser & Visser, *supra* note 155, at 60.

184. Kettell, Nutshell, *supra* note 171, at 210.

185. Visser & Visser, *supra* note 155, at 60.

186. Hassan & Lewis, *supra* note 1, at 52.

187. Brian B. Kettell, The Islamic Banking and Finance Workbook: Step-by-Step Exercises to help you, 80 (John Wiley & Sons Ltd., 2011).

188. *Id.*

189. Venardos, Islamic Banking, *supra* note 82, at 59. See also Hassan & Lewis, *supra* note 1, at 50.

190. Venardos, Current Issues, *supra* note 75, at 176.

191. Alexei Kireyev, Financial Reforms in Sudan: Streamlining Bank Intermediation, 45 (International Monetary Fund, Issues 2001-2053) (2001).

192. *Id.*

193. *Id.* at 43.

194. *Id.* at 45.

195. Brian Kettell, Nutshell, *supra* note 171, at 219.

196. Venardos, Current Issues, *supra* note 75, at 176.

197. Munawar Iqbal & David T. Llewellyn, Islamic Banking and F inance: New Perspectives on Profit Sharing and Risk, 98 (Edward Elgar Publishing, 2002).

198. *Id.* at 93.

199. *Id.* at 102.

200. *Id.* at 93.

201. Greg N. Gregoriou and Paul Ali, The Credit Derivatives Handbook: Global Perspectives, Innovations, and Market Drivers, 19 (The McGraw Hill Companies, Inc. 2008).

202. Iqbal& Llewellyn, *supra* note 198, at 93. *See also* Venardos, Current Issues, *supra* note 75, at 67.

203. Venardos, Current Issues, *supra* note 75, at 175.

204. Iqbal & Llewellyn, *supra* note 198, at 98. *See also* Venardos, Current Issues, *supra* note 75, at 67.

205. Iqbal & Llewellyn, *supra* note 198, at 98. *See also* Venardos, Current Issues, *supra* note 75, at 67.

206. Iqbal & Llewellyn, *supra* note 198, at 98.; *See also* Venardos, Current Issues, *supra* note 75, at 67.

207. Simon Archer, Rifaat Ahmed Abdel Karim, Islamic Finance: the Regulatory Challenge, 315 (John Wiley & Sons (Asia) Pte. Ltd., 2007).

208. Iqbal & Llewellyn, *supra* note 198, at 98.

209. *Id.* at 95.

210. Venardos, Islamic Banking, *supra* note 82, at 59. *See also* Hassan & Lewis, *supra* note 1, at 52.

211. Iqbal & Llewellyn, *supra* note 198, at 95.

212. *Id.* at 98.

213. *Id.*

214. Simon Archer, Rifaat Ahmed Abdel Karim, Islamic Finance: The Regulatory Challenge, 337 (John Wiley & Sons (Asia) Pte. Ltd., 2007).

215. *Id.* at 315.

216. Hassan & Lewis, *supra* note 1, at 52.

217. Shujat Ali Baig, "Growth Constraints in the Financial Sector, " *Inpaper Magazine*, July 4, 2011. *See also* http://www.dawn.com/2011/07/04/comment-and-analysis-growth-constraints-in-islamic-financial-sector.html

218. *Id.*

219. *Id.*